INTRODUCTION TO MEDIEVAL LOGIC

INTRODUCTION
TO
MEDIEVAL LOGIC

ALEXANDER BROADIE

CLARENDON PRESS · OXFORD
1987

Oxford University Press, Walton Street, Oxford OX2 6DP
Oxford New York Toronto
Delhi Bombay Calcutta Madras Karachi
Petaling Jaya Singapore Hong Kong Tokyo
Nairobi Dar es Salaam Cape Town
Melbourne Auckland
and associated companies in
Beirut Berlin Ibadan Nicosia

Oxford is a trade mark of Oxford University Press

Published in the United States
by Oxford University Press, New York

British Library Cataloguing in Publication Data
Broadie, Alexander
Introduction to medieval logic.
1. Logic, Medieval
I. Title
160'.9'023   BC34
ISBN 0–19–824941–1

Library of Congress Cataloging in Publication Data
Broadie, Alexander.
Introduction to medieval logic.
Bibliography: p.
Includes index.
1. Logic, Medieval.   I. Title.
BC34.B76   1987   160'.9'023   86–23552
ISBN 0–19–824941–1

Typeset by Hope Services, Abingdon, Oxon
Printed in Great Britain
at the University Printing House, Oxford
by David Stanford
Printer to the University

Contents

I

Introduction

There can be no doubting the central role accorded logic in the educational scene in the Middle Ages. There are two related aspects to this role, one institutional and the other scientific. The first is that at the heart of the medieval educational system were the seven liberal arts, divided into the trivium, three arts ·of language, and the quadrivium, four mathematical sciences. The arts of the trivium, the so-called 'trivial arts', were grammar, rhetoric, and logic, and during a period of several centuries practically every university graduate had received a training in those arts. The second aspect of the role of logic explains the first. Logic was referred to, and indeed was generally regarded, as 'the art of arts and the science of sciences', for the study of it was considered a propaedeutic to all the other sciences. The great English logician William of Sherwood said of grammar, rhetoric, and logic that they teach us respectively to speak correctly, ornately, and truly. As regards logic, part of what he had in mind was that logic is a tool with whose aid we could reach the truth by a rational investigation of what is already known to be true. That is, logic would prevent us slipping from truth to falsehood. Considered in this light it was bound to be concluded that there was no person who could not benefit from a training in logic, for truth is a goal we all by our very nature seek.

One distinction commonly drawn now, though not explicitly drawn by medieval logicians, is that between philosophical and formal logic. The distinction is however useful for present purposes, since each of those two heads of division picks out a great deal of material found in the medieval logic textbooks. Philosophical logic is a philosophical enquiry which takes as its subject certain concepts of particular concern to the logician. Thus, for example, logic can be characterized, sufficiently for immediate purposes, as the systematic study of valid inference. Let us say, provisionally, that an inference is valid if it is impossible for its premisses to be true without the conclusion being true. That definition naturally prompts certain questions. For example can any light be shed on the concept of truth invoked in our definition?

And in ascribing truth, what is it to which it is ascribed? Is it, perhaps, the proposition considered as an utterance or inscription, or is it the proposition considered as the sense of the utterance or inscription? Or is the bearer of truth value something different from any of these things? These questions and others also prompted by the above definition of validity are philosophical and are not to be answered by a logician working solely within the bounds, however loosely conceived, of formal logic.

Formal logic, on the other hand, presupposes either that we already know the answers to the above questions, or at least that we have an insight into the answers which is sufficient for the needs of formal logic, and proceeds to the question of the identification of the rules of inference which can then be used to test inferences for validity.

Most of those who made a significant contribution to logic in the Middle Ages were philosophers just as much as they were logicians, and in most cases they were as much at home on the philosophical as on the formal frontier of logic. Their philosophical researches illuminated the logic, and their logical researches underpinned the philosophy. The philosophy led naturally to an investigation of the rules governing valid inference, for philosophers, committed as much as anyone could be to rational enquiry, had to be able to defend their arguments against charges of invalidity. And some of their philosophical enquiries were themselves prompted by consideration of the rules of logic. I shall be attending in the following pages to their ideas on both philosophical and formal logic.

The high point of logic in the Middle Ages was the fourteenth century, and it is on the writings of that period that most of what is said in this book will be based. But those writings had great forerunners and great successors, and my net will be cast sufficiently wide to take in the writings of earlier logicians and also of later ones, even considerably later ones. For in the decades before the Reformation important discoveries were being made in logic by men who were very much part of the medieval logical and philosophical world. However, the logicians upon whom I shall be drawing most heavily are Walter Burley, William Ockham, John Buridan, Albert of Saxony, and Paul of Venice, universal thinkers of the fourteenth century.

2

Aspects of Language

I. *Terms, propositions, inferences*

At the heart of logic is the concept of an inference or argument. For present purposes the question of what makes an inference valid is secondary. What does concern us immediately is the obvious fact that any inference is complex. And the nature of that complexity has to be attended to. For before we can say which inferences are valid we first have to be able to identify certain things as inferences, and inferences have a characteristic complexity for every inference is composed of propositions. At least two are required since one is to be understood to follow from the rest. And every proposition is itself complex for, as Aristotle said, it must have at least two parts, a noun and a verb. Nouns and verbs were traditionally classed as terms. And this gives us three levels of complexity, first, terms, then propositions, which are composed of terms, and finally inferences, which are composed of propositions. This way of putting the matter suggests an obvious order of exposition for the logician. Since terms are the elements out of which propositions are composed, they should be examined first, and inferences, as composed of propositions, should be examined last.

Other approaches are possible, and indeed might be thought preferable. For example, at least as regards some terms it is commonly held that they can be explained only by reference to the way in which they, as elements in propositions, contribute to the validity or otherwise of inferences. Thus a standard way to expound 'and' is to say that given two propositions, P and Q, then the proposition 'P and Q', which results from conjoining P and Q, implies P, and it implies Q, but neither P by itself nor Q by itself implies the conjunctive proposition. It might indeed be argued that it is impossible to explain 'and' without describing its role in valid inferences. Likewise it could be said that 'every' cannot be explained except by reference to such considerations as that 'Every A is B' implies 'Some A is B' but not vice versa. According to this approach it may seem that it is not the least complex, but the most complex, namely the inference, that should be the starting-point.

Medieval logicians, however, began their logic textbooks, at least those of their textbooks containing comprehensive accounts of logic, by considering terms first, and then reaching their study of inferences by way of an analysis of propositions. But all the same it should be said that their order of exposition should not be taken to signify that they would have rejected the notion that terms, or at least some terms, are inexplicable except by reference to the role they play in valid inferences. On the contrary, their practice shows that they accepted this point.

There is a sense in which modern formal logic, expounded axiomatically, accords with medieval practice. For modern axiomatic systems characteristically begin by specifying the elements out of which propositions can be composed, and classifying those elements. They then specify those combinations of elements which are permissible, that is, which form propositions (well-formed formulae), and finally they specify the rules by which a proposition may be inferred from a given set of propositions. The difference between medieval practice and modern is therefore, at least in this respect, not as great as might at first be supposed.

That practice is traceable to Aristotle, and indeed the traditional ordering of the books which constitute his contribution to logic reflects the ordering: terms, propositions, inferences. For of that set of books, known as the *Organon* (= 'tool' or 'instrument'), the first, the *Categories*, is concerned with terms and their classification. The second, *De Interpretatione*, is concerned with propositions and their classification, and the remaining books, the *Prior* and *Posterior Analytics*, the *Topics*, and the *Sophistical Refutations*, are concerned with the rules of valid inference and with the classification of arguments good and bad.

II. *Terms*

I shall follow the traditional order of exposition and begin with the notion of a term, and since a term is a kind of sign I shall take the concept of sign as my starting-point. William Ockham refers us to two notions of sign. He writes '[A sign is] anything which, when grasped, makes something else come to mind, though what is brought to mind is not in the mind for the first time but is actually in the mind after being known dispositionally' (*Summa Logicae*, I 1). Thus, for example, a barrel hoop outside a tavern is a sign of wine, and the utterance 'William' is a sign of William. This sense of 'sign' is said to be a wide sense. The second sense, presumably narrower, is as follows: 'A sign is that which makes something come to mind and is fitted by its nature to stand for that thing in a proposition, or to be added to what stands for that thing in a proposition . . . or is fitted by its nature to be composed of such things' (*Summa Logicae*, I 1). He has in mind here nouns and nominal phrases, which stand for things in the context of a proposition, and words such as 'is' and 'every' and 'not', which can be added to such expressions, and finally, propositions, which are composed of expressions of the kinds just mentioned. It is not clear precisely what Ockham took to be the relation between the wide and the narrower senses of 'sign', but to call them wider and narrower is probably itself misleading since it is not certain that everything which is a sign in the narrower sense is also a sign in the wider sense. For it is probable that a sign in the wider sense is something which stands for something. Certainly Ockham's examples suggest this interpretation. But Ockham frequently said of many expressions which are signs in the second sense, for example, 'is' and 'every', that they neither do nor can stand for anything. However, whatever the nature of the relation between these two senses of 'sign' it was with the second, narrower, sense that Ockham was chiefly concerned, and it is with that sense that we shall be concerned hereafter.

A language is a system of signs, and those signs can be ordered roughly according to their relative complexity. Terms are signs, so are propositions, and so are inferences. The word 'term' was defined in a variety of ways by medieval logicians, and indeed one logician might offer several definitions on a single page. Perhaps the commonest definition was 'a proximate part of a proposition'. Elucidation of this phrase was provided by reference to Aristotle: 'I call a term that into which a proposition is resolved, namely, a predicate and that of which the predicate is predicated, when it is affirmed or denied that something is or is not the case' (see Aristotle, *Prior Analytics*, 24b16–18, and e.g. Ockham, *Summa Logicae*, I 1). According to this account a term is a subject or a predicate of a proposition, whether an affirmative or a negative proposition. Thus, for example, in 'A young man is reading a book' the subject 'a young man' and the predicate 'reading a book' are both terms.

The sample proposition just used has the form of a categorical proposition since it consists of a subject, a predicate, and a coupling device or 'copula', 'is', linking subject with predicate. The three parts of the categorical proposition, viz. subject, predicate, and copula, were commonly referred to as the principal parts of the categorical proposition, and this notion of the principal parts of such a proposition also provided a definition of 'term'. Thus 'A young man is reading a book' was said to contain three terms.

Other definitions of 'term' were also given, and no one of them came to be treated as the principal one. But this wealth of definitions of 'term' rarely caused confusion, since it was in general quite clear which concept of 'term' the logician had in mind when he predicated the word of a linguistic expression. It is, however, plain at least that whatever concept the logicians were seeking to capture they were not primarily, if at all, aiming to encapsulate in a definition of 'term' our concept of 'word'. But all the definitions of 'term' have this much in common, that they all imply that a term is a significative part of a proposition, even though they do not all imply that every significative part of a proposition is a term.

Sufficient for our immediate purposes has now been said about the nature of a term, and I should like to turn to a consideration of a crucial principle of division of terms.

III. *Thoughts, utterances, inscriptions*

In a passage of great importance for the development of medieval logic, Aristotle writes:

Now spoken sounds are symbols of affections in the soul, and written marks symbols of spoken sounds. And just as written marks are not the same for all men, neither are spoken sounds. But what these are in the first place signs of—affections of the soul—are the same for all; and what these affections are likenesses of—actual things—are also the same. (*De Int.* 16a3–8)

In due course these words were appropriated for a wide range of purposes. St Thomas Aquinas, for example, used the first sentence of the foregoing passage as a starting-point for his argument for the claim that words do not signify entirely differently when applied to God and to his creatures (*Summa Theologiae* 1a,13,1,c). Something should be said here about that sentence, for it was given an interpretation that at first sight seems ill suited to the words. Aristotle appears to be envisaging a quadrilateral of relations between an inscribed word, an uttered word, a thought (an 'affection of the soul'), and a thing: say, the inscription 'man', the utterance 'man', the thought of a man, and a man, and to be saying that the inscription 'man' signifies the utterance 'man', the utterance signifies the thought of a man, and the thought is a likeness of a man. On this interpretation the utterance directly signifies not a man but a thought of a man. What directly signifies a man is the thought. But this account of the significative function of inscriptions and utterances has the consequence that if a person writes or says 'A man is reading', he is signifying that it is either the utterance 'man' or the thought of a man that is reading. This theory of the relation between inscriptions, utterances, thoughts, and things is plainly nonsense, and a different interpretation of Aristotle's position was given and generally accepted, namely, that an inscription and an utterance signify a thing no less immediately than does a thought. But it was added that in a sense the thought signifies primarily what the utterance or inscription signifies secondarily. We see something, and in so doing we naturally form a thought of that thing. Until we have the thought we cannot use any sound or mark to signify the thing. Once we have the thought, a convention can be established whereby a sound or mark has the signification that the thought has by nature. Thus what the utterance and inscription signify depends on our thought, but the signification of a thought does not depend on utterances or inscriptions. Thus thoughts have this kind of priority over inscriptions and utterances; but if we choose to call this a priority of signification, that is not to be understood to mean that the inscription and the utterance do not signify the thing as directly as does the thought.

In his commentary on the Aristotelian passage under discussion, Boethius asserts that there are three kinds of speech (*oratio*), namely, written, spoken, and conceived or thought speech, and that there are correspondingly three kinds of term. Written speech is visible, spoken speech is audible, and conceived or thought speech is not available to any of the five external sensory modalities but exists in the intellect only and therefore exists only as thought (*In Librum De Interpretatione*, 2a, I, cap. *De Signis*. See *Patrologia Latina*, 64, 407B). We have observed that there is a certain relation of subordination of written and spoken terms to thoughts, and staying with Boethius's tripartite classification of language I should like to specify some of the chief differences between these sorts of language. Aristotle will, on this matter as on many others, be our guide.

He asserts that 'affections of the soul' are the same for all men, but utterances and inscriptions are not. Let us stay with this point. Spoken and written signs are in an obvious sense conventional. That we use the sounds or marks we do use in order to communicate is not a fact of our nature, for we could have used other signs, and other nations do use other signs. But what I think of when I think of what I call a 'man' is the same as what a Frenchman thinks of when he thinks of an 'homme', and as what a Greek thinks of when he thinks of an 'anthropos'. The thought is the same though the conventional expression of it differs. Thus the language of thought is universal in contrast to what we may term the 'parochiality' of conventional languages. Indeed, the intertranslatability of conventional languages is due precisely to the fact that, different as they are in respect of many of their characteristics, they can all be used to express the same set of thoughts. In contrast with the conventionality of written and spoken languages the medieval logicians spoke of the language of thought as a natural language, a language we have by our nature. The term 'natural' is misleading for us in this context since it is customary to speak of English, Latin, etc. as natural languages, as contrasted with artificial languages such as Esperanto. But I shall continue to use the terminology of the medieval logicians. My practice in this matter will be constant so should not lead to misunderstanding.

Each of us has a cognitive faculty, that is, a set of abilities, to understand, to calculate, to intuit. And these were thought of as part of our natural endowment. A change occurs in us when we think, for we are different at least in respect of the thoughts we have that we had previously not had. A change, however, to what? The commonest answer was that the cognitive faculty undergoes modification. Let us suppose that you say to me 'A man is reading.' My cognitive faculty is modified by the very fact of my grasping what you have said. But that modification is itself an act of understanding. And it should be said that my cognitive faculty is modified in exactly the same way when someone says to me 'Homo legit' or 'Un homme lit.' What this suggests, as the medieval logicians saw clearly, is that when we think, we do not think in any of the conventional languages, even though we cannot express what we think without using one of those languages.

If the foregoing points are correct a problem arises concerning the obvious question of how, if at all, we spell the terms in the mental language. I think that a man is reading, and I say what I think in English. How many letters has the mental term which corresponds to the spoken term 'man'? The answer cannot be 'three', since that mental term is identical to the mental term corresponding to the spoken Latin term 'homo' and to the French 'homme'. But if a term has any letters it surely has a determinate number. The conclusion drawn was that mental terms differ from conventional terms in this, among other things, that they are not composed of letters. An important corollary of this is that a conventional term can change its signification but a mental term cannot. Change implies a permanent underlying the change. In the case of conventional terms the permanent is the string of letters in the inscription or the string of sounds in the utterance. But a mental term, conceived of as a modification of a cognitive faculty, cannot change its signification for there is nothing to it over and above the signification. The mental term can cease to exist and does so when the mental act, which is what the term really is, ceases. But the mental term cannot lose one signification and gain another, for there is nothing by which it could be identified as the same mental term again, lacking as it does anything corresponding to letters or sounds.

Several logicians raised the question of the extent to which mental language corresponds to conventional languages. William Ockham, for example, held that mental language contains nouns, verbs, and prepositions, singularity and plurality, but that it makes no distinction between the different declensions of nouns (*Summa Logicae*, I 3). It seems to have been the opinion of Albert of Saxony that mental language does not make a distinction between nouns and pronouns (see *Perutilis Logica*, 3rb). Also it was commonly held that mental language does not contain synonymous terms, that is, distinct terms with the same signification. The last point is readily understandable, for there is no way of distinguishing mental terms which do not differ in respect of their significations if in fact there is nothing to them except those very significations.

That mental language does not distinguish between the declensions of nouns is also readily understandable, for declensions are distinguished by systematic differences in spelling. And by the same token there is no distinction in the conjugation of the different verbs. Indeed it makes no sense to ascribe declensions and conjugations to mental nouns and verbs, given that mental terms contain no letters.

Those elements in a conventional proposition to which there are corresponding elements in the corresponding mental proposition are the significative elements which make a contribution to the truth value of the conventional proposition. That is the chief reason logicians were interested in mental language, the language of thought. A distinction was commonly made between those features of language of interest to the logician and those of interest to the grammarian. Some grammatical features of a proposition interested the logician, for instance the distinction between subject and predicate, the tense of verbs, the singularity or plurality of nouns, the case of nouns, for all these have an effect on the truth or otherwise of the propositions containing the terms in question. But that the subject of a proposition is of the first declension rather than the second can make no contribution to the truth value of the proposition, assuming that the subject has its customary signification. Thus when the logician set out to determine whether a given inference was valid, his procedure in effect was to determine how the inference would appear in mental language, and then to establish the validity or otherwise of that mental inference. The mental inference would be the conventional inference shorn of all those of its features that made no contribution to the truth value of the premisses and conclusion or to the validity or otherwise of the inference.

Medieval logicians did not devise a fully symbolic logic, but in the main investigated inferences which were couched in Latin, a living language. They wanted to know which inferences expressed in that language were valid. To do this they first had to lay bare the logical forms of the propositions in the inferences, the logical, not the grammatical forms. And to do this they asked themselves what it was that they thought when they thought the inferences which were then expressed in conventional language. In other words, they investigated the natural language of thought as the only means available to them to discover the rules of valid inference. It is, then, not at all surprising that the concept of mental language was such a central concept for the medieval logicians.

IV. *The temporality of propositions*

So far propositions have been classed under one or other of three headings, as mental, spoken, or written. As we saw, the difference between spoken and written propositions is that the former are audible and the latter visible. St Augustine, indeed, asserted that there were propositions graspable by the other senses also: 'Of the signs with which men communicate with each other some belong to the sense of sight, and fewer to that of hearing, and fewest to the other senses' (*De Doctrina Christiana*, Bk. II). But let us stay for the moment with utterances, inscriptions, and thoughts. It was a characteristic doctrine of medieval logic, and one upon which a great deal hinged, that propositions are either thoughts, or are visible or audible expressions of thoughts. For from this it follows that it makes sense to speak of a proposition as coming into existence and ceasing to exist, as for example, when someone thinks something and then ceases to think it, or when someone writes something down and the inscription is erased.

There is a modern view to the effect that a proposition is the sense of a sentence, perhaps specifically an indicative or an assertoric sentence. And some hold that propositions as so conceived have a life of their own which is quite independent of the sentences which express them. That is, it is held that propositions as so conceived can exist even if the corresponding thoughts, utterances, or inscriptions do not exist and have never existed. There is room for doubt over whether this is a viable theory, for any sense is the sense of an expression, and if there is no expression for the sense to be a sense of we might wonder whether the sense itself can exist. But however this difficulty should be resolved, we should note that this way of considering propositions is as far removed as could be from the way revealed in very many medieval logic textbooks.

The medieval view that a proposition has a time-span and also, in the case of inscriptions, a spatial location, plays a role right at the heart of medieval logic in discussions about the nature of valid inference. For if we say that an inference is invalid if it is possible for the premisses to be true without the conclusion being true, then many inferences which we should regard as valid would have to be classed as invalid on the grounds that the premisses might be true at a time when the conclusion does not exist at all and in that case is not at that time true.

I do not wish to take this problem further here; it will be considered again later. I wish at this stage merely to stress that for the rest of this book when I speak of propositions, I mean propositions understood as having the kind of existential status ascribed to them by medieval logicians. And given the relation between propositions and terms, it follows, as a corollary of what has just been said, that whatever existential status is ascribed to propositions must also be ascribed to the terms out of which the propositions are composed.

v. *Terms: categorematic and syncategorematic*

I have spoken of the medieval logicians as engaged, at least as a major part of their task, in identifying the logical form implicit in propositions. It was recognised that terms of a certain class played a particularly important role in the task of identification, and in this section I should like to focus on that class of terms.

Medieval logicians were accustomed to make a distinction between significative and non-significative terms. The latter are what we should now call nonsense words. The former are all the other words, that is, every word which has a signification. Within the class of significative terms a distinction was made. Paul of Venice writes:

A term significative per se is one which, taken by itself, represents something, for example 'man' or 'animal'. A term which is not significative per se is one which, taken by itself, represents nothing, for example, 'every', 'no', and such like. (*Logica*, pp. 1–2)

This passage sheds light on a further passage which occurs some lines later:

Of terms some are categorematic and some are syncategorematic. A categorematic term is one which, by itself and also with another term, has a proper significate, for example 'man'. Whether it is placed in a sentence (*oratio*) or placed outside one it always signifies a man. A syncategorematic term is one with a function, which taken by itself is significative of nothing, for example, universal signs such as 'every', 'no', and the like; and particular signs, for example, 'some', 'a certain', etc., prepositions, adverbs, and connectives. (ibid.)

One point made by Paul of Venice is that the fact that a term is significative does not imply that it signifies something, though it is true of some terms that they are fitted by their nature to signify things. For example, the term 'man' signifies something, namely, a man. And even if as a matter of fact no man exists the term is still fitted by its nature to signify something. It is not, as it were, the term's fault that there is no man for it to signify. A term with such a nature is called a categorematic term. A syncategorematic term is a significative term which is not categorematic. Paul instances 'every', 'no', and several others. When he says that they have a function he has in mind the fact that they play a distinctive role in the context of a proposition, and that their signification is to be defined in terms of that distinctive role. For example, William of Sherwood says that the function of the word 'every' is to divide the subject in relation to the predicate, so that in the proposition 'Every man is an animal' the 'every' functions in such a way that the proposition implies that this man is an animal, and that man is an animal (and so on for all men). (See his *Syncategoremata*, p. 48.)

Another syncategorematic term is the verb 'be' and its various forms. Clearly it signifies nothing, but does have a function in a proposition, most especially to connect two categorematic terms, namely, the subject and the predicate, in a proposition. Further syncategorematic terms are 'and', 'or', and 'if'. It is evident that the class of syncategorematic terms contains almost all, if not all, the terms that we should think of as the special preserve of the logicians.

Some of the terms classed as syncategorematic and extensively investigated were those called exponible terms. An exponible term is, roughly, one of interest to the logician and in need of exposition or clarification. The reason a later generation of logicians gave for this need was the obscurity of the term. Not all logicians included 'every' in their class of exponible terms, though some did. But amongst the terms which were generally included were 'begins' and 'ceases'. In one respect it is plain that these terms should be classed as syncategorematic, for they are auxiliary verbs exponible in terms of tensed copulas. Thus 'A begins to be B' means 'Immediately before now A was not B and now A is B, or now A is not B and immediately after now A will be B'. But the matter is not entirely plain sailing. One late-scholastic logician, David Cranston, describes the terms 'begins' and 'ceases' as categorematic exponibles (*Term.* b vii). What he appears to have in mind is that the terms 'begins' and 'ceases' are grammatically simple but logically complex, and in particular that our conventional language conflates two terms of logically quite distinct natures. For 'begins' and 'ceases' can be seen each to contain a part of the verb 'to be' plus a categorematic term. Thus 'begins' is subordinate to a mental expression which is represented more perspicuously by 'is beginning' or 'is a beginner'. And one might then say that 'begins' is categorematic in virtue of implicitly containing 'beginner' and is syncategorematic in virtue of implicitly containing 'is'.

Amongst other things this last example illustrates the way the medieval logicians set about their task of investigating the logical form implicit in conventional propositions. 'A man begins' appears to have two parts, a noun and a verb, and grammatically speaking it does. But logically it was taken to have three parts, a subject, copula, and predicate, that is, a syncategorematic and two categorematic terms. And the principal reason why the form had to be made explicit was that the rules of valid inference were so formulated that they could be applied only to inferences whose premisses and conclusion had all been written in a form which was an adequate representation of the form of the mental propositions to which they were subordinate. Thus given the rule that if every B is C and every A is B it follows that every A is C, we can argue that 'Every beginner is substantial and every man is a beginner. Therefore every man is substantial' is a valid inference, but we cannot even apply the rule to 'Every beginner is substantial and every man begins. Therefore every man is substantial', and certainly we cannot on the basis of the rule judge the inference valid, for the second premiss is of the wrong form.

3

Truth Conditions of Categorical Propositions

I. *Propositions: categorical and molecular*

'Proposition' was commonly defined in terms of truth. Paul of Venice, for example, following a long tradition, said that a proposition is 'indicative speech signifying something true or something false' (*Logica*, p. 4). For an item of speech to signify something true or something false that item must have an appropriate logical form. Such forms were extensively investigated, and were generally expounded in a recursive manner. That is, a given form was specified as minimally sufficient if the item of speech was to be able to signify something true or something false, and other forms were described in terms of operations carried out on items of speech which could signify something true or something false. As regards the minimal form, we have already met that. It is the categorical proposition, composed of just three parts, subject, copula, and predicate, for example, 'A man is reading.' Operations can be carried out on such a proposition transforming it into a more complex item of speech still able to bear a truth value. For example, it can be universalized by prefixing 'every' to the subject: 'Every man is reading.' It can also be negated by placing 'not' before the subject or before the predicate. The propositions resulting from such transformations are as categorical as the proposition thus transformed by the addition of the syncategorematic terms. Thus 'Not only every man is not reading' is categorical.

But there are other propositions, described as molecular, which do not have the basic logical form: subject plus copula plus predicate. A molecular proposition is any pair of propositions connected by a syncategorematic term taken from a precisely enumerated list of terms. But though many logicians gave a list, they did not all list the same terms. However, every list included at least 'and', 'or', and 'if'. Two propositions connected by 'and' formed a conjunctive proposition, by 'or' formed a disjunctive, and by 'if' a conditional proposition. Each proposition thus connected could be categorical, and one or both could be molecular. Hence, a molecular proposition could contain 'and', 'or', and 'if', all connecting propositions. Whether the resulting proposition is conjunctive, disjunctive, or conditional depends on what the principal connective is. If, say, the proposition is composed of a disjunction connected to a conditional by 'and', the proposition is a conjunction. It was well recognized that where a molecular proposition contained several propositional connectives of distinct kinds it was the order of construction of the proposition that determined what kind of molecular proposition it was. Thus, given three propositions P, Q, and R, the molecular proposition 'P and Q or R' was said to be conjunctive if it was formed by placing 'and' between the two propositions 'P' and 'Q or R'. And it was said to be disjunctive if it was formed by placing 'or' between 'P and Q' and 'R' (see Burley, *De Puritate*, p. 108).

At the beginning of his treatise on molecular propositions, Paul of Venice refers to the disparity in the length of the lists of propositional connectives drawn up by different logicians (see *Logica Magna*, 124va). Some, he reports, list five. He probably had in mind William Ockham who, in addition to the three so far mentioned, listed causal and temporal connectives. 'Since' is a sign of causality. Thus, 'Since Socrates does not wish to be ignorant Socrates philosophizes' is given as an example of a causal proposition. 'When' and 'while' are temporal connectives, as in 'Plato listens when (or while) Socrates speaks' (see *Summa Logicae*, II 30). Others, Paul adds, list six propositional connectives. One who did so was Albert of Saxony, who gave Ockham's list with the addition of the sign of locality. 'Where' is such a sign, as in 'Socrates is where Plato is' (see *Perutilis Logica*, 19ra). Another source, reports Paul, lists seven propositional connectives. He may have had in mind a text called *Ars Emmerana* (*c.*1200), which lists all the connectives so far mentioned plus the sign of adjunction, that is, 'in order that' (see L. M. de Rijk, *Logica Modernorum*, II 2 158–9). But Paul of Venice eventually accepts the view, stated also by Peter of Spain, that there are just three kinds of molecular proposition, namely, conjunction, disjunction, and conditional. It might be said, for example, that temporal and local propositions are to be classed as conjunctions, on the gounds that, for example, 'A is when B is' and 'A is where B is' are equivalent to 'A is and at the same time B is' and 'A is and in the same place B is' respectively. But whether or not Paul's arguments for rejecting the claims that there are more than three kinds of propositional connective are sound, I shall, for the purpose of expounding the theory of truth conditions as that theory was applied to molecular propositions, restrict myself to consideration of the three kinds sanctioned by Peter of Spain and Paul of Venice. Those three kinds of molecular proposition received much the greatest coverage in medieval discussions of molecular propositions.

II. *Supposition: personal, simple, material*

Two statements by Aristotle lie behind a good deal of medieval theorizing about truth conditions. Aristotle affirms: 'To say of what is that it is not, or of what is not that it is, is false, while to say of what is that it is, and of what is not that it is not, is true' (*Meta.* 1011b26), and 'The true judgment affirms where the subject and predicate really are combined, and denies where they are separated' (*Meta.* 1027b20). The first of these two statements has universal application for it sets no limit on the kind of proposition which can be judged true or false, whereas the second account of truth and falsity is relevant only to categorical, and not at all to molecular propositions. We shall begin with the latter of the two statements, and shall expound it in terms of the concept of supposition.

Supposition is the signification that a certain kind of term has in the context of a proposition. The definition that John Buridan gives is representative:

Supposition is the taking of a term in a proposition for some thing or some things such that when that thing or those things are pointed to by the pronoun 'this' or 'these' or their equivalent, then that term is truly affirmed of that pronoun with the copula of the proposition mediating. (*Sophismata*, b 5)

It is clear from this that only a categorematic term can have supposition, for no term can supposit that is not fitted to be a predicate. Let us say that a given categorical proposition contains a term T. That term supposits for something such that we can pick the thing out with the demonstrative pronoun 'this' and say truly 'This is T.' Wherein, then, lies the difference between supposition and the signification of a categorematic term, for the latter seems to answer to the description just given of supposition? An important part of the answer can be given by reference to the example of the term 'man'. This term signifies everything such that we can point to it and say truly 'This is a man.' As regards the term 'man' as it occurs in the proposition 'A man is reading', its supposition is the same as its signification. In the context of that proposition the term 'man' stands for something such that we can point to the thing and say truly 'This is a man.' The situation is, however, quite otherwise as regards the proposition 'Man is a species', for in the context of that proposition 'man' does not stand for what it stands for in 'A man is reading.' A species is not the kind of thing that can read even if the members of it are of that kind. That the term 'man' has different significations in the context of the two propositions is made plain by the fact that this argument 'Every man is seated. A man is reading. Therefore a reader is seated' is valid, but this 'Every man is reading. Man is a species. Therefore a species is reading' is invalid. What has gone wrong in the second of these two inferences is that the so-called fallacy of equivocation has been committed, for in the first premiss the term 'man' signifies an individual man and in the second it does not. There is considerable room for dispute regarding the manner of existence of species as opposed to the members of the species. But among the logicians with whom we are concerned the general consensus was that a species is a concept (or mental term) under which we bring the members of the species. This is a version of the theory known as nominalism, as contrasted with realism which states that species are real things which exist apart from thought. Whichever formulation of the nominalist position we adopt, the outcome is that the term 'man', used to signify a species, does not signify what it customarily signifies, namely, individual men.

Terminology was coined to mark the distinction of the kind which we have made between the two uses of 'man'. When a term T in the context of a proposition signifies what it customarily signifies so that T stands for or, so to say, personates the thing, then it is said to have personal supposition. If T does not have its customary signification but signifies a mental term, in particular the mental term which stands for the thing that T customarily signifies, then T is said to have simple supposition.

A third kind of case was distinguished. In the proposition ' "Man" is triliteral' the term 'man' is evidently not intended to stand for an individual man, for it is senseless to say that a man, say, Socrates, is triliteral. And neither does the term stand for the species man, for the species is a mental term, and we have already observed that mental terms are not composed of letters and hence cannot be triliteral. Clearly 'man' is intended to stand for the very word 'man' itself, considered as an inscription. The three letters m, a, and n are the material out of which the inscription is composed. And since in ' "Man" is triliteral' the subject stands for 'man' in respect of the material out of which it is composed, the term is said to have material supposition in the context of that proposition.

It was commonly said that a term with material supposition stands for itself in the context of the proposition. Sometimes it was added that it also stands for anything equiform to itself (*consimilis sibi*). The point is that the term 'man' in ' "Man" is triliteral' does not stand only for the very occurrence of 'man' in the subject place of the inscription just inscribed. It stands for any occurrence of the inscription 'man', that is, for the occurrence of any term equiform to the term in the subject place of our sample proposition.

In the fourteenth century most logicians recognized these three kinds of supposition. Subsequent generations reduced the list to two by conflating the categories of simple and material supposition on the ground that in each case what the term in question stands for is not what the term customarily signifies, but instead it stands for the term itself, whether considered as a mental term or as an utterance or an inscription.

So far we have considered only the supposition of the subjects of propositions, but predicates supposit also. Supposition is, after all, the signification that a term has in the context of a proposition. It is the 'taking the place (*positio*) of another thing' in the context of a proposition (see Ockham, *Summa Logicae*, I 63). And this is a role that a predicate, no less than a subject, plays. But whereas a subject can have personal, simple, or material supposition, a predicate has just personal supposition. For example, in ' "Man" is triliteral' the predicate stands in the context of that proposition for what it customarily signifies, namely, something which is triliteral. Assuming that the proposition is true, then which triliteral thing the predicate stands for in that context is given by the subject. And in 'Man is a species' the predicate stands for what it customarily signifies, namely, a species. Assuming that the proposition is true, then which species it is that the predicate stands for in the context of that proposition is given by the subject.

As to the problem of determining the kind of supposition possessed by the subject the solution is to consider the predicate with which the subject is coupled. Ockham (*Summa Logicae*, I 65) lays down the general rule that whatever the proposition in which a given term be placed, that term can have personal supposition unless those who use the term restrict it to a different sort of supposition. But a term cannot have simple or material supposition in every proposition, but only in a proposition where the term is linked to an extreme (presumably the predicate extreme rather than the subject) which refers to a mental term or to an utterance or inscription. For example, in 'A man runs' the subject term must have personal supposition since 'runs' cannot refer to a mental term or to an utterance or inscription. And since 'species' signifies a mental term, 'man' in 'Man is a species' can have simple supposition. If it does have simple supposition then the proposition is true. If it has personal supposition the proposition is false.

For the remainder of this chapter our attention will be focused on personal supposition. That was the kind of supposition in which medieval logicians were particularly interested. And their writings on that topic are particularly rich in logical insights.

III. *Personal supposition*

Categorematic terms were considered under two headings, for of such terms some are discrete, or singular, and some are common. The distinction is of great importance for the development of the theory of supposition. A discrete term is one which is fitted by its nature to signify one and only one thing. The proper name 'Socrates', for example, is a discrete term. That as a matter of fact a given term does signify only one thing is not by itself proof that the term is discrete. The term 'sun' was not considered discrete, for though as a matter of fact there was (as it was thought) only one sun, that was an accidental fact about the world and not a fact that could be deduced from a consideration of the mode of signification of the term. The question to answer, then, is not: Is there one and only one sun? but rather: Is the term 'sun' fitted by its nature to signify one and only one thing? Proper names are not the only kind of discrete term. Even though a given common term is not discrete, that term prefixed by a singular demonstrative term is discrete. Thus 'man' is not a discrete term but 'this man' is.

A term is common if it is fitted by its nature to stand for many things. 'Man' is common. Even if there is only one man the term is none the less common since it is an accidental fact about the world and not a fact which can be learned from a consideration of the mode of signification of the term. Indeed, a term may be common though there is in fact nothing for which it stands. The stock medieval example was 'chimera', a mythical beast whose existence was thought a physical impossibility. 'Chimera' was classed as a common term since the term was fitted by its nature to stand for many things. That fact about the mode of signification of the term is the only relevant fact in establishing whether or not the term is common.

Supposition was considered under two heads, discrete and common. Discrete supposition is the supposition possessed by a term signifying discretely in the context of a proposition. Thus in 'Socrates is reading' the subject has discrete supposition. In ' "Socrates" is a proper name' the subject term does not have discrete supposition, for though 'Socrates' is fitted by its nature to stand for one and only one thing, nevertheless in the context of that proposition the term has material supposition. It stands for the name 'Socrates'. And there could be many occurrences of that name. In 'This man is reading' 'man' has discrete supposition because in the context of that proposition it stands for one and only one man, namely, *this* one. Thus whether the supposition of a term is discrete does not depend simply on whether the term is in any case a discrete term, it depends on whether it is discrete in the context of the proposition.

Common supposition is the supposition possessed by a term which, in the context of the proposition, has common signification. Thus in 'A man is reading' the subject term has common supposition. In 'A Solomon is sitting in judgement' the proper name has common supposition, since in the context of the latter proposition the subject stands for someone with exceptional qualities as a judge, and many could have such qualities.

Medieval logicians did not on the whole attend a great deal to discrete, as compared with common, supposition. It was not in the least that they considered discrete supposition to be comparatively unimportant, but rather that there was simply much more to be said about common supposition. Let us, then, turn to the notion of common supposition in order to see what the notion yields up about the logical form of propositions.

Common supposition was considered under two headings, determinate and confused. We shall examine determinate first. Consider the proposition:

(1) Some man is a logician.

It was standardly held that an affirmative categorical proposition is false unless the subject and predicate stand for something, not in the sense that they are fitted by their nature to stand for something, but in the sense that there actually is something such that the subject can be truly predicated of a demonstrative pronoun indicating that thing, and there actually is something such that the predicate can be truly predicated of a demonstrative pronoun indicating that thing. Thus in the case we are considering we should have to say that (1) is false unless there is a man, for if there is no man then there is no man to be a logician in which case it is not true that some man is a logician. And likewise if there is no logician then it cannot be true that some man is a logician. So the medieval position concerning the existential implications of affirmative categorical propositions seems sound. But as regards the truth conditions of (1) it has to be added that there should be some particular man, man^n, such that the predicate of (1) can be truly predicated of 'man^n'. Hence, given (1) this follows:

(2) Man^1 is a logician or man^2 is a logician, and so on for every man.

So (1) implies a disjunction of singular propositions, each disjunct of which is like (1) except that the common term in the subject place of (1) is replaced by a singular term of which the common term is truly predicated. Medieval logicians spoke of this relation between (1) and (2) as a descent under the subject to a disjunction of singular propositions. Descent was classed as a form of valid inference. It can easily be shown that descent can also be made under the predicate of (1) to a disjunction of singular propositions. Additionally (1) follows from any one of the disjuncts in (2). That is, ascent can be made from any one of the singulars to the original proposition. A term under which such descent and such ascent can be made was said to have determinate supposition.

We turn now to confused supposition. This is the kind of supposition possessed by any term which has common supposition but does not have determinate supposition. There are two kinds, confused distributive and merely confused. We deal with the first kind first. If the following proposition:

(3) Every man is mortal

is true then this proposition:

(4) Man^1 is mortal and man^2 is mortal, and so on for every man

is also true. Here descent is made under the subject of (3) to a conjunction of singular propositions. But ascent cannot validly be made from any one of the conjuncts to the original proposition. Where descent can be made under a given term to a conjunction of singular propositions but ascent cannot be made from any of the conjuncts then the term is said to have confused distributive supposition.

Finally we turn to merely confused supposition. Let us stay with (3). (3) implies the following:

(5) Every man is mortal^1 or mortal^2, and so on for every mortal.

That is, descent can be made under the predicate term of (3) to a proposition like (3) except that the predicate of (3) is replaced by a disjunction of singular terms of each of which the predicate in (3) can truly be predicated. And additionally if it were true that every man was mortal^n, as would be the case if there were only one man and he were mortal, then (3) would be true. Here ascent is made from one of the singular terms under the original term. Where such descent and such ascent can be made under a given term then that term is said to have merely confused supposition.

Numerous rules were given for determining the kind of personal supposition that terms possessed. We shall briefly rehearse certain of the more important of these rules. They were hedged about with qualifications, but I shall pay little attention to those. One rule is that a term covered by no syncategorematic term has determinate supposition, as also has a term immediately covered by 'some' and not also covered by a sign of negation. Secondly a term covered immediately by a sign of universality, for example, by 'all' or 'every', has distributive supposition, and one covered mediately by a sign of affirmative universality has merely confused supposition. A term is mediately covered by a given sign if the term comes at the predicate end of a proposition whose subject is immediately covered by the sign. Thirdly, a term covered, whether immediately or mediately, by a sign of negation has confused distributive supposition (hereinafter just 'distributive supposition'). Thus in the universal negative proposition 'No man is immortal', both the subject and the predicate have distributive supposition, and in the particular negative proposition 'Some man is not a logician', the predicate has distributive supposition and the subject has determinate supposition.

It is plain that in many categorical propositions the subject and the predicate do not have the same sort of supposition, and a question arises regarding the order in which descent should be made under subject and predicate. To see what is at stake here we can note briefly the following example. In:

(6) Some man is not a logician

the subject has determinate and the predicate distributive supposition. If we descend first under the predicate and assume there to be not more than two logicians, we reach the proposition:

(7) Some man is not logician^1 and some man is not logician^2.

And it is clear that that is consistent with every man being a logician. Indeed, so long as there are at least two men, (7) must be true because it cannot be that each man is every logician. Hence (6) does not imply (7), and yet it should do if the descent is correctly made under the predicate term. The error consisted in descending under the term with distributive supposition before descending under the term with determinate supposition. Assuming there to be not more than two men, what (6) implies is this:

(8) Man^1 is not a logician or man^2 is not a logician.

We can now descend under the distributed predicate to reach the following:

(9) Man^1 is not logician^1 and man^1 is not logician^2, or man^2 is not logician^1 and man^2 is not logician^2.

Stated briefly the rules said to govern the order of descent are as follows: determinate supposition has priority over distributive and merely confused supposition, and distributive supposition has priority over merely confused.

Given the syntactic rules presented earlier for determining the kind of supposition possessed by a given term, it follows that changing the position of a term in a proposition can have an effect on the truth value of that proposition. In:

(10) Every teacher has a pupil

'pupil' has merely confused supposition, and consequently the proposition says that this teacher has some pupil or other and that teacher has some pupil or other, and so on for every teacher. But in:

(11) A pupil every teacher has

'pupil' now has determinate supposition, and since 'teacher' has distributive supposition descent must be made first under 'pupil' and then under 'teacher'. Assuming there to be just two teachers and two pupils, the first stage of descent takes us to:

(12) Pupil¹ every teacher has or pupil² every teacher has.

The next stage takes us to:

(13) Pupil¹ teacher¹ has and pupil¹ teacher² has, or pupil² teacher¹ has and pupil² teacher² has.

This latter proposition implies that some one pupil is shared by all the teachers, and that is plainly not implied by (10), though it does imply (10). It was by such means that medieval logicians dealt with what is now known as the quantifier shift fallacy, that is, the fallacy committed when arguing, for example, that if every action aims at some good, then there must be some good, i.e. one and the same good, at which all actions aim.

Concern for order of terms in a proposition emerges often in the medieval logic textbooks, and the chief point at issue is the effect that a change in order might have on the kind of supposition a term has. Thus Albert of Saxony quotes the rule: 'A term which includes a negation in itself gives distributive supposition to the following term' (*Perutilis Logica*, 13ra), and instances the term 'differs', presumably because it has the same signification as 'is not the same'. Hence in:

(14) Socrates differs from a man

'man' is distributed, and consequently (14) signifies that Socrates differs from every man, i.e. that there is no man that Socrates is. Albert contrasts this with:

(15) Socrates from a man differs

for in (15) man has determinate supposition, and hence (15) implies that it is from man¹ that Socrates differs or from man², and so on for all men. It is in virtue of the different kinds of supposition possessed by 'man' in (14) and (15) that the former proposition is false and the latter true. And on the basis of the same considerations it can be shown (to adapt one of Albert's examples) that:

(16) Socrates differs from Plato

implies (15) but not (14) even though Plato is a man, for in (14) 'man' signifies every man and in (15) it signifies this man or that man, etc.

Likewise it was commonly held (see e.g. Albert of Saxony, *Perutilis Logica*, 13rb) that terms expressing comparison have a similar effect to negation signs. Let us say that in a proposition of the form 'A is Xer than B' 'A' is the excedent and 'B' the excessum. Then it was held that the term expressing comparison gives distributive supposition to the following excessum. Thus in:

(17) Socrates is stronger than a man

'man' has distributive supposition, and hence (17) is false since it implies that Socrates is stronger than every man—including himself. But the rule applies to the following excessum, not to a preceding one. If, therefore, we wish to say that Socrates is stronger than a man, i.e. than at least one man, without wishing to imply that he is stronger than every man, the way to do this is to transfer the excessum to a position before the comparative term, for example:

(18) Socrates than a man is stronger.

We have so far considered cases of terms giving distributive supposition to a succeeding term. I should like now to consider a different type of case. Let us stay with Albert of Saxony's exposition. He asserts that some terms have the power to give merely confused supposition to terms following them. Examples of such terms are the verbs 'seek', 'desire', 'promise', and 'owe' (see *Perutilis Logica*, 13vb). Hence in:

(19) I promise you a penny

'penny' has merely confused supposition, as it has in:

(20) I owe you a penny

and as has 'horse' in:

(21) For riding there is required a horse.

Let us stay with (19) and consider the effect on its truth conditions of placing 'penny' before the verb, as in:

(22) A penny I promise you.

Here 'penny' has determinate supposition. That is, (22) implies:

(23) This penny I promise you or that penny I promise you

(assuming, for the sake of simplicity, that there are only two pennies in existence). That is, there is some particular penny that I promise you. Yet that is not at all what (19) says, for (19) says that I promise you some penny or other, though no penny in particular, and hence I discharge my debt to you by giving to you a penny, no matter which of the available pennies it is. If in fact the truth is sufficiently expressed by (19), then if I give you a penny in order to discharge my debt, you cannot say truly that I have not discharged my debt for I have given you the wrong penny. Nothing counts as the wrong penny, for any penny will do as well as any other. As Albert of Saxony puts the point, (19) is consistent with:

(24) No penny I promise you.

But this matter is not entirely plain sailing. Albert argues as follows: Let us suppose that Socrates promises to pay Plato a penny and that Socrates then gives him a penny. We can fairly ask whether Socrates did or did not give to Plato what he had promised him. If the answer is affirmative then since it was penny A that Socrates gave him it must have been penny A that Socrates promised him, and therefore not only did Socrates promise Plato a penny but also there was a penny that Socrates promised Plato. If, however, the answer is negative, then Socrates still owes Plato what he promised him, and he might give Plato a hundred or a thousand pennies and still not fulfil the promise. It seems, then, that whenever A promises B an X it is some X in particular that A promises B.

But Albert does not accept this. He takes the view that in promising Plato a penny Socrates does not promise him some penny in particular. Though of course the penny he gave was a particular penny, it was not that penny in particular that was promised. That penny in particular is used to discharge the debt, but it is not in virtue of being that penny in particular that it can discharge the debt, but in virtue of its being any penny. It is only if Socrates gives neither penny A nor penny B, and so on for all pennies, that the debt would not be discharged. 'And so', concludes Albert, 'it is possible that someone owes another person something and yet there is nothing that he owes him' (*Perutilis Logica*, 14ra).

Albert adds the following parallel for good measure:

Likewise it follows that I need an eye for seeing, and yet there is not some eye that I need for seeing. For I do not need the right eye since I can see with the left, nor the left eye since I can see with the right. But that I need an eye to see with is true, since if I had only one eye then there is an eye I would need for seeing.

The foregoing points should be read in the light of the distinction made by William of Sherwood to which we referred near the start of Chapter 1, namely, that between rhetoric and logic. Latin is highly flexible as regards word order, very much more so than English, and a Roman orator or poet could pick one word order rather than another on the basis of likely psychological impact. But the medieval logicians were forging a scientific Latin, a Latin much freer from ambiguity than ordinary everyday Latin was. They had no interest in elegance, only in truth and in whatever serves the truth. And truth is well served by a language in which the truth can be unambiguously expressed. What the logicians did was fix on certain orderings of words as having a specific logical significance. They were not reporting established linguistic practice. They were fixing rules which, if followed by philosophers and theologians, would contribute to a greater mutual understanding, and hence would provide conditions in which the truth was more likely to emerge from the dialectical process.

A final point is in order here. The preoccupation with the ordering of terms in a proposition was no greater among medieval logicians than it is among their modern successors. In general, whether an existential quantifier precedes or follows a universal quantifier makes a difference to the truth conditions of the propositions containing those quantifiers. In an idiom appropriate to their epoch medieval logicians made a very similar point, made it with great clarity, and pursued its implications with rigour.

IV. *Negation*

While on the topic of categorical propositions I should like to make certain points about negation. It is appropriate to consider the matter here since the negation sign functions, among other things, as an operator forming a categorical proposition out of a categorical proposition. But a distinction has to be made here, for the two principal kinds of linguistic unit with which we have so far been concerned are the term and the proposition and medieval logicians recognized that the negation sign can serve as an operator covering each of these kinds of sign. Let us consider briefly the medieval concept of term negation.

Such negation was termed 'infinitizing negation'. The 'not' or 'non' infinitizes the term which it covers. We shall use 'non' as our term negating sign. Thus, given the categorematic term T, another term 'non-T' can be formed. 'Non-T' is also categorematic, and stands for everything for which T does not stand and for nothing for which T does stand. The number of non-chairs in a given room is the number of things minus the number of chairs. Such a negation added to a singular term results in a common term ('non-Socrates' is common since it is fitted by its nature to stand for many things—namely everything which is not Socrates). Whether that negation added to a common term results in a common or a singular term depends on what the negation is added to. Added to 'chair' the result is another common term. But there is a law of double negation for terms. What it states is that given any term T, the negated negation of T signifies precisely what T signifies. Consequently the negated negation of a singular term must signify precisely what that singular term signifies. 'Non-non-Socrates' is fitted by its nature to signify just Socrates. And hence a doubly negated singular term is itself a singular term. But what the first negation in the string negates is itself a common term. It must be concluded, therefore, that an infinitized common term is not necessarily a common term. Whether it is a common term or not depends on whether the categorematic term to which the string of negation signs is prefixed is common or not. If it is common its double negation is common, and if singular its double negation is singular.

To appreciate the significance of certain rules of valid inference, it is important to note that the presence of a negation sign in a proposition is not sufficient to justify classifying the proposition as negative. For the presence of an infinitizing negation does not result in a negative proposition. Hence the rule of syllogistic inference, that at least one premiss must be affirmative, is not violated by a syllogism merely in virtue of its having a negated term in each premiss. Nevertheless, it was commonly held that a proposition containing a negated term is equivalent to a proposition composed of two or more categorical propositions none of which contains a negative term. For example, Ockham asserts that 'A donkey is a non-man' is equivalent to 'A donkey is something and a donkey is not a man' (*Summa Logicae*, II 12). The reason why 'A donkey is a non-man' is not said to be equivalent to 'A donkey is not a man' is that an affirmative categorical proposition is not true unless both the subject and the predicate stand for something, and hence 'A donkey is a non-man' implies the existence of a donkey and of a non-man. But it was held that a negative categorical proposition is true if either the subject or the predicate term does not stand for anything, and hence 'A donkey is not a man' is true if there are no donkeys. In the light of these considerations it is not surprising to find Ockham denying that 'A chimera is a non-man' is equivalent to 'A chimera is not a man.' For him the former proposition is false, and the latter is true. Indeed it has to be concluded, as Ockham notes, that a chimera is no more a non-man than it is a man. Put otherwise, 'A chimera is a man or a chimera is a non-man' is false (necessarily false given the view that it is impossible for there to be any chimeras), but 'A chimera is a man or a chimera is not a man' is necessarily true.

Medieval logicians developed a number of puzzles based on the ambiguity that arises when it is possible that a given negation negates either the proposition or the term. Thus 'Non terminus est terminus' can mean either 'It is not the case that a term is a term' or ' "Non-term" is a term' or 'A non-term is a term.' We shall not delay over these puzzles, whose flavour it is in any case difficult to recreate in English, but shall focus on an offshoot of them. Where the negation sign occurs at the start of a proposition and is followed immediately by a common noun it is often difficult to determine, at any rate in the case of a Latin proposition, which of the two roles, outlined above, the negation sign has in that context. But it should be noted that a negation sign does not infinitize a term unless it is prefixed immediately to that term, whereas a proposition can be negated by a negation sign which does not occur at the start of the proposition, but occurs in the middle of it, or even at the end. The following are all negative propositions:

(a) Not every man is a logician
(b) Every man is not a logician
(c) Every man a logician is not.

In accordance with medieval practice, (a) should be classified not as a universal proposition but as a particular—the result of negating a universal affirmative proposition was said to be a proposition neither universal nor affirmative. But (b) and (c) are both universal. More important, however, is the fact that the three propositions all differ in their truth conditions. In (a) the subject has determinate and the predicate distributive supposition; in (b) both extremes have distributive supposition; and in (c) the negation sign has no effect on the supposition of either extreme since it follows both of them. The subject has distributive supposition and the predicate determinate supposition. Assuming there to be just two men and two logicians, and using A and B as abbreviations for 'man' and 'logician' and ~ for 'is not', the truth conditions for the above three propositions are respectively:

(a1) $(A^1 \sim B^1$ and $A^1 \sim B^2)$ or $(A^2 \sim B^1$ and $A^2 \sim B^2)$
(b1) $(A^1 \sim B^1$ and $A^1 \sim B^2)$ and $(A^2 \sim B^1$ and $A^2 \sim B^2)$
(c1) $(A^1 \sim B^1$ and $A^2 \sim B^1)$ or $(A^1 \sim B^2$ and $A^2 \sim B^2)$

Put otherwise, (a) is true if there is something for which 'man' stands for which 'logician' does not stand. (b) is true if there is no one thing for which 'man' and 'logician' both stand. And (c) is true if there is something for which 'logician' stands for which 'man' does not stand.

On the basis of the principles so far outlined it is easy to work out the truth conditions of the foregoing three sample propositions if 'every' is replaced by 'some'. Since no new issue of principle is involved I shall not give the details here, but shall turn instead to an examination of the truth conditions of propositions where new issues of principle do arise.

v. *Past, present, future*

We have so far considered a highly restricted range of categorical propositions and I should like now to extend that range considerably. For, first, truth conditions have so far been specified only for present-tensed propositions and there is good reason to suppose that additional considerations have to be brought into play if the truth conditions of past- and of future-tensed propositions are to be sufficiently expounded. And secondly, we have restricted our attention to so-called 'propositions of inherence'. A proposition of inherence is a non-modal proposition. A modal proposition is one expressing possibility, necessity, impossibility, or contingency. Some logicians would add to that list. But I shall for the present deal only with the foregoing modalities. We should therefore ask what the truth conditions are for modal propositions.

Let us deal first with propositions about the past and the future. Given that the truth condition of 'A man is a logician' is that there is something for which 'man' and 'logician' both stand, it might seem that the truth condition of 'A white thing was black' is that there is something for which 'white' and 'black' both stood, or perhaps that there was something for which 'white' and 'black' stood. But neither of these suggestions is plausible, and neither was canvassed by medieval logicians. 'A white thing was black' might be true because what is now for the first time white had up to this moment been black. And in that case the claim that the proposition is true cannot be justified on the

ground that there is something for which 'white' and 'black' stood, for
by our hypothesis 'white' did not stand for what 'black' stood for,
though it now stands for what 'black' stood for. And by the same token
the claim that it is true cannot be justified on the ground that there was
something for which 'white' and 'black' stood.

Of course, 'A white thing was black' might be true though there is
now nothing that is white. It would be sufficient for the truth of the
proposition that there was something for which 'white' stood and
'black' stood. It is evident from these points that in the context of the
proposition, 'white' cannot be taken to signify simply something which
is white or simply something which was white. The tense of the copula
causes an extension—medieval logicians called it an 'ampliation'—of
the signification of the subject term to that which is or that which was.
So Albert of Saxony, following the common line, asserts: 'This
proposition "A white thing was black" signifies that that which is white
or that which was white was black' (*Perutilis Logica*, 15rb). There is not
however a corresponding extension or ampliation of the predicate. Its
relation to the past-tensed copula ensures that the predicate signifies
what was black. The implication of this is that the truth conditions of
our sample proposition can be given as follows: 'This is white' is or was
true, and 'This is black' (said while indicating the same thing as that
indicated by the demonstrative pronoun in 'This is white') was true.
There is ample evidence that this represents the kind of approach
taken by medieval logicians to the question of the truth conditions of
past-tensed propositions. Thus, for example, Ockham raises the
question of the truth conditions of 'A white thing was Socrates', given
that 'white thing' supposits for what is white, and he answers: 'It is not
necessary that this was at some time true: "A white thing is Socrates",
but it is necessary that this was true: "This is Socrates", said while
indicating that for which the subject supposits in "A white thing
was Socrates" ' (*Summa Logicae*, II 7).

The reason why it is incorrect to say that the truth condition of 'A
white thing was black' is given by 'This was true: "A white thing is
black" ' is that the latter proposition implies that something was white
and black simultaneously, whereas the sample proposition does not
imply that. But a distinction should be made here between a past-
tensed categorical proposition whose subject is a common term and
one whose subject is a proper name. For in contrast with the previous
sample proposition, Walter Burley states that the proposition 'Socrates
was white' has a truth condition which can be stated simply as this:

' "Socrates is white" was true' (*De Puritate*, p. 48). For whereas if a white thing was black, it could not have been white while it was black, if Socrates was white then he must have been Socrates while he was white. He need not then have been *called* 'Socrates', but as John Mair points out: 'Socrates is not Socrates because he is called "Socrates". He was in fact Socrates before that name was imposed to signify that thing' (*Term.* 12ra). But it does not follow from this that in order to state the truth conditions of a past-tensed proposition whose subject is a proper name it is sufficient to replace the past-tensed copula by the corresponding present-tensed copula and then say of the duly transformed proposition that it was true. One obstacle to such a manœuvre is that the original past-tensed proposition might have a time specification besides the pastness of the copula. For example, as regards Ockham's proposition 'Socrates was white yesterday' it is clearly unacceptable to give its truth condition as: ' "Socrates is white yesterday" was true.' The obvious tactic in dealing with such a proposition is to remove the time specification from the original proposition and place it in the form of words used to make an ascription to the duly rewritten past-tensed proposition. In accordance with that prescription the truth condition of 'Socrates was white yesterday' is given by: ' "Socrates is white" was true yesterday.'

There is clear evidence in all this of the adoption of a recursive procedure in giving the truth conditions of propositions. Present-tensed non-modal propositions were dealt with first. And once the means for identifying the truth conditions of such propositions had been established, the means for establishing the truth conditions of past-tensed propositions could be specified. Such means involved, essentially, rewriting the past-tensed proposition in the present tense and placing the past-tense features of the original proposition in a predicate within whose argument place the rewritten present-tensed proposition was placed. In general, the question of the kind of supposition possessed by terms was not raised for terms as they occurred in the past-tensed propositions but only as they occurred in the present-tensed rewrite of the past-tensed propositions.

The identification of the truth conditions of future-tensed propositions was not on the whole thought to raise problems of a different kind from those involved in identifying the truth conditions of past-tensed propositions. With obvious changes the account to be given can be read off the account given in this section of the truth conditions of past-tensed propositions. I shall therefore not discuss future-tensed propositions here, but shall turn briefly, in the next section, to the interesting question of the truth conditions of modal propositions. The excursion into modal logic will have the additional advantage of introducing us to terminology which will be of importance in the next chapter.

VI. *Modal propositions*

At the start of this chapter two accounts of truth, both taken from Aristotle's *Metaphysics*, were given. In the last section it became plain that those accounts failed if applied, without adaptation, to past- or future-tensed propositions. The point I wish to make here is that, unless adapted, they also fail if applied to propositions expressing possibility, necessity, impossibility, or contingency. For example, the proposition 'A man can be a logician' is true, but it is not thereby true that, to use Aristotle's phrase, 'the subject and predicate really are combined.' For if they are really combined then a man is, and not merely can be, a logician. A standard medieval interpretation of Aristotle's accounts of truth was this: 'Every true proposition is true because, howsoever the proposition signifies, so it is in the thing signified or in the things signified' (see e.g. Buridan, *Cons*. a ii). And Buridan, noting the need for an adaptation, affirms: 'This is true: "Something which never will be can be", not because things are as the proposition signifies, but because things can be as the proposition signifies they can be' (*Cons*. a ii). For the remainder of this section we shall be considering the implications of this position.

It was common to distinguish between a categorical proposition and the dictum of the proposition. In Latin the dictum of a proposition is formed by replacing the subject of the proposition by its accusative form, and replacing the finite main verb by its infinitive form. I shall use the standard 'that' clause construction to render the Latin accusative plus infinitive construction. Thus the dictum of 'A man is an animal' is 'that a man is an animal'. One way to construct a modal proposition is to predicate a modal term of a dictum. Ockham gives the example: 'That every man is an animal is necessary' (*Summa Logicae*, II 9). And he argues that the truth condition of that proposition is that the proposition corresponding to the dictum is necessary. That is, 'That every man is an animal is necessary' is true just if the proposition 'Every man is an animal' is necessary. And similarly for a dictum of which 'possible', 'impossible', or 'contingent' is predicated.

But Ockham adds an important rider, namely, that:

As regards a necessary proposition it should be noted that it is not because the proposition is always true that it is necessary, but because if it exists it is true and cannot be false. For example, this mental proposition 'God exists' is necessary, not because it is always true—for if it does not exist it is not true—but because if it exists it is true and cannot be false. (*Summa Logicae*, II 9).

He held likewise that an impossible proposition is impossible not because it is always false, but because if it exists it is false and cannot be true. The implication, though not stated explicitly by Ockham, is that a proposition is possible not because it is sometimes true but because its existence does not imply its falsity.

Where a modal operator includes within its scope, or covers, an entire proposition or dictum, the proposition containing the modal operator is said to be a modal proposition 'with composition' (*in sensu composito*). The examples we have so far considered are of this kind. Where the modal operator covers a part, but not the whole, of a proposition then the proposition is said to be a modal proposition 'with division' (*in sensu diviso*). In such cases the modal term divides the proposition into two parts, the part not covered by the term, and the part covered by it. In the light of our earlier discussion on the way the position of a negation in a proposition was held to affect the truth conditions of the proposition, it comes as no surprise to discover that Ockham and others held that the place of a modal term in a proposition can have an effect on the truth conditions of the proposition. As we observed, it was said that 'That every man is an animal is necessary' is true if the proposition 'Every man is an animal' is necessary. But 'Every man is necessarily an animal' is true if there exists something for which 'man' stands, and 'This is an animal' is necessary, for every man indicated by 'this'. (Ockham did not accept that 'Every man is necessarily an animal' is true, for he held that 'This is an animal' is not necessary, whatever is indicated by 'this'. For whatever is an animal has merely contingent being, and therefore this (which is an animal and which *is* contingently) is contingently whatever it is, and hence it is contingently an animal).

The general rule is this: 'A is modally B', where 'modally' holds a place for 'necessarily', 'possibly', etc., is true just if the mode expressed in such a proposition is truly predicated of a non-modal proposition in which B is predicated of a pronoun indicating that for which A stands. For example, of 'Every truth is necessarily true', Ockham gives the following truth condition: 'This is true' is necessary, for every truth indicated by 'this'. And in that case, he concludes, 'Every truth is necessarily true', is itself false. There are, after all, propositions which, though true, are only contingently so. In contrast Ockham does not argue against 'That every truth is true is necessary', presumably because he saw it as an instance of the law of identity, that is, that everything is itself. (The common rejection of 'Every chimera is a chimera' and 'A chimera is a chimera' is not incompatible with the law of identity formulated as above, for though everything is itself, no chimera exists and hence no chimera is anything—and hence no chimera is itself.)

Because Ockham accepts this account of the truth conditions of propositions which are modal with division, he accepts that 'A white thing can be black' is true. For the latter proposition is true if the following condition is satisfied: There is something for which 'white' stands, and 'This is black' is possible where 'this' indicates something for which 'white' stands. Were the sample proposition to be understood to mean 'That a white thing is black is possible' it would, of course, have to be rejected as false, since the proposition corresponding to the dictum 'that a white thing is black' is contradictory.

'Can' and 'possible' are ampliative. They extend the supposition of the subject to cover what is and what can be. But if the subject in 'A white thing can be black' stands for what is or can be white, then the truth condition, given in the preceding paragraph, is not the only one that that proposition would satisfy. For the earlier truth condition specifies that there is something for which 'white' stands, whereas the sample proposition is consistent with there being nothing for which 'white' stands so long as there can be such a thing. Assuming that white things do not exist though they can, then 'A white thing can be black' is true if the following condition is satisfied: This is possible: 'A white thing can be black' where 'white' stands for something which is white. And this condition is itself satisfied by the truth condition given in the previous paragraph (see *Ockham's Theory of Propositions*, ed. Freddoso and Schuurman, p. 58).

There is a metaphysical aspect to the above account of the truth conditions of propositions of possibility. 'A can be B' does not imply the attribution of B to something with possible being, as though possibly being is a way of being, and is a way of being which involves having sufficient being to have the attribute B. The Ockhamist line is that when it is said that A is possibly B, or can be B, where A does not but can exist, the modality must be understood to be predicated of one or more non-modal propositions, and should not be understood to qualify the existence of A itself. To Ockham, at least, it seemed plain that if A does not exist, then its existence does not have the quality of possibility.

4

Truth Conditions of Molecular Propositions

1. *Conjunction*

At the start of the previous chapter brief reference was made to molecular propositions. We shall now examine that topic in detail. It was stated earlier that there was little agreement on the question of how many kinds of molecular proposition there are. But that lack of agreement was not a reflection of disagreement about the basic conditions that have to be satisfied if a proposition is to be classed as molecular. A molecular proposition is a proposition containing several categorical propositions. Such a proposition also contains, whether explicitly or implicitly, a connective (often called a *copula*), or even several connectives if the connective after which the particular molecular proposition takes its name connects propositions of which at least one is also molecular. A molecular proposition was said to be 'simple' if it contained just two categorical propositions, and 'composite' if at least one of the propositions connected by the principal connective was itself molecular. We shall for the most part attend to simple molecular propositions. While 'and', 'or', and 'if' were the most commonly investigated propositional connectives, it should be said that each one of these terms was also examined in respect of its role as a connective between categorematic terms as well as between propositions. Let us take the term 'and' first.

Paul of Venice provides useful terminology:

A sign of conjunction is sometimes taken conjunctively and sometimes conjointly. It is taken conjunctively when it connects categorical propositions, and it is taken conjointly when it unites terms only. An example of the first kind is 'Socrates runs and Plato moves'. An example of the second kind is 'Socrates and Plato run'. (*Logica Magna*, 127vb)

And in addition, a sign of conjunction taken conjointly can itself be distinguished in terms of what follows from the proposition containing it. The sign 'is taken divisively when from a proposition of which it is a part there follows a conjunctive proposition composed of equiform terms. It is taken collectively when no such conjunctive proposition follows' (ibid.). For example, 'and' occurs as conjoint and divisive in 'Socrates and Plato run', since (i) the 'and' connects two terms, and (ii) the proposition implies the conjunctive proposition 'Socrates runs and Plato runs.' Paul's example of a proposition containing 'and' functioning collectively is 'Socrates and Plato are sufficient to lift stone A.' As he says, that they can, between them, lift it does not imply that each alone could do so. A good deal of effort went into the identification of the rules by which on syntactic grounds it could be established whether a given conjoint 'and' was functioning divisively or collectively. We shall not pursue that tortuous line of enquiry here, but shall instead attend to 'and' where it is conjunctive.

The truth conditions of a conjunction are easily stated: 'For the truth of a conjunction it is sufficient and necessary that all its principal parts, between which the conjunction is the connective, are true' (Burley, *De Puritate*, p. 110), and correspondingly it is false if either principal part is false (Albert of Saxony, *Perutilis Logica*, 19^{rv}).

The truth conditions of a proposition in which possibility is predicated of a conjunction can be stated almost as simply: That a given conjunction of propositions is possible is true if (i) each of the conjuncts is possible, and (ii) the two conjuncts are mutually compossible (Burley, *De Puritate*, p. 111). Hence for a conjunction to be impossible it is sufficient that it have two conjuncts, both possible, which are mutually incompossible, as in Burley's example: 'Socrates is white and Socrates is black.' It is also sufficient that either of the parts be impossible. These two conditions together form the necessary and sufficient conditions for the impossibility of a conjunction. The notion of incompossibility is immediately invoked by Burley to resolve a problem about valid inference. It is a rule of valid inference that the impossible does not follow from the possible, and yet the impossible 'A black thing is white' follows from the two premisses 'Socrates is white' and 'Socrates is black.' As Burley points out, each of the premisses is possible, but they are not compossible, and from incompossible premisses an impossible proposition can be concluded without infringing any law of logic.

Paul of Venice considers a more complicated kind of case than does Burley. Paul gives as a sufficient condition for the possibility of an affirmative conjunction that each principal part be compossible with each, or with all the others at the same time, if there are more than two. He gives two examples, of which the first is obvious enough: 'Some man is every runner and Socrates is a runner and Plato other than Socrates is a runner.' As Paul points out the first part is compossible with the second and with the third, and the second is compossible with the third, but the first is not compossible with the other two combined, nor the second with the first and third combined. The other, rather more interesting example is: 'Into these parts continuum A is divided and into these parts continuum A is divided and so on to infinity.' Each part of this conjunction is compossible with each other part. But they are not all mutually compossible because of the impossibility of an actually infinitely divided continuum. Had the sample proposition contained 'divisible' rather than 'divided' the proposition would not have been found unacceptable. (See *Logica Magna*, 129vb.)

In the light of remarks made in the previous chapter about the truth conditions of past-tensed propositions, a word should be said about a doubt that Burley raises in connection with the identification of the truth conditions of conjunctions. It was commonly held that a proposition, containing a conjoint subject followed by a part of the verb 'to be' and no predicate, was equivalent to a conjunctive proposition with parts equiform with the first proposition, for example, 'Socrates and Plato are' and 'Socrates is and Plato is.' But Burley argues that whereas 'Adam was' and 'Noah was' are both true, 'Adam and Noah were' is false, and therefore 'Adam was and Noah was' does not imply 'Adam and Noah were'. His argument for the claim that the latter proposition is false is that 'every true past-tensed proposition at some time was true in the present-tense' (*De Puritate*, pp. 111–12). If 'Adam and Noah were' is true then at some time in the past 'Adam and Noah are' was true. But the latter proposition never was true since Adam and Noah were never alive simultaneously. This position may seem odd. Burley himself offers the counter-argument that 'Adam and Noah were' is true since Adam is dead and Noah is dead also. Neither of them, therefore, is, though both were, that is, Adam and Noah were. He appears to accept this last argument. At any rate he accepts the conclusion, and to the former argument he offers the following objection:

For the truth of a past-tensed proposition where an act is signified by a plural verb, it is not necessary that it have some present-tensed version which at some time was true, but it is sufficient that it have several present-tensed versions which at some time were true. So 'Adam and Noah were' has these two present-tensed versions 'Adam is' and 'Noah is', which were at some time true. (*De Puritate*, p. 112)

Such a set of truth conditions for a proposition consisting of a conjunction of proper names followed only by a past-tensed part of the verb 'to be' clearly has the desirable consequence of ensuring that if the bearer of each of the names was, then both bearers were.

II. *Disjunction*

There was no dispute amongst our logicians that the sign of disjunction should count as a propositional connective, though there was certainly dispute regarding the truth conditions of disjunctive propositions. We shall reach the nub of the dispute shortly. First it should be noted that a certain distinction we made regarding the function of 'and' should also be made regarding 'or'. In each case what has to be noted is that the connective can connect either two terms or two propositions. Following our earlier distinction between 'and' in its conjoint and its conjunctive employment, we must make a distinction between 'or' in its disjoint and its disjunctive employment. In 'You are a man or a donkey', 'or' is disjoint. In 'You are a man or you are a donkey', 'or' is disjunctive. And just as 'and' can be either divisive or collective, so 'or' can be one or other of these. Paul of Venice explains: 'It is taken divisively when the argument from any part of the disjoint term to the disjoint term, and from the disjoint term to a disjunctive proposition with equiform terms is sound' (*Logica Magna*, 131^{rb-va}). He gives two examples: Since 'You are a man. Therefore you are a man or a donkey' is sound, the disjoint 'or' in the conclusion is divisive. And likewise, since 'Socrates or Plato runs. Therefore Socrates runs or Plato runs' is sound, the disjoint 'or' in the premiss is divisive. A disjoint 'or' occurs collectively when neither of these conditions is satisfied. Paul's examples are 'or' in 'I am different from you or from me', since the proposition does not follow from 'I am different from you', and the 'or' in 'You know that a king sits or that no king sits', since that proposition does not imply 'You know that a king sits or you know that no king sits.' The disjoint 'or' will be of concern to us chiefly in so far as it is used divisively, that is, in so far as the proposition containing the disjoint 'or' either implies or is implied by a disjunctive proposition.

As regards the truth conditions of a disjunctive proposition there were two main opinions. Walter Burley attributes to the great Augustinian theologian Giles of Rome (*c.*1243–1316) the view that a necessary condition for the truth of a disjunctive proposition is that one of the disjuncts be true and the other false. For, as Boethius says, the sign of disjunction between the disjuncts does not permit them to be (i.e. to be true) simultaneously (see *De Puritate*, p. 115). Giles's conception just outlined is of what we should now call 'exclusive disjunction', a disjunction in which affirmation of either disjunct excludes affirmation of the other, or, put otherwise, in which each disjunct implies the negation of the other. But Giles's was a minority opinion. The standard position was that the sufficient and necessary condition for the truth of a disjunction is that at least one of the disjuncts be true. The falsity of either disjunct does not imply the falsity of the disjunction, but the truth of a disjunct does imply the truth of the disjunction. The way the matter was commonly stated was that the truth of either part of the disjunction is by itself a sufficient cause of the truth of the disjunction, and therefore the truth of the two disjuncts together is a cause of the truth of the disjunction. This conception of 'or', the 'inclusive' conception, is the one we shall assume to be employed in subsequent examples of propositions with disjunctive occurrences of the term.

Peter of Spain adopted an awkward compromise position between the minority and the majority views. He asserts that for the truth of a disjunction it is sufficient that one or the other part be true, and adds: 'It is permitted that both parts be true, though this is a less proper use' (*Tractatus*, pp. 9–10). But this statement of position is unsatisfactory from the logical point of view, as the following generation of logicians recognized. For they were engaged in the construction of a scientific Latin in which, most especially, the role of every logical term was precisely defined so that the truth conditions of propositions containing those terms could be stated precisely. Thus, for example, a logician wished to know precisely what the truth conditions of a disjunction were. He was not helped by knowing what Peter of Spain told him, namely, that there was a more appropriate and a less appropriate role for 'or', even if he knew what the more and the less appropriate roles were. For additionally he needed to know, for each occurrence, which role the 'or' was performing.

Given the truth conditions, stated above, for disjunctive propositions, the falsity conditions can easily be deduced. For granted that the necessary and sufficient condition for the truth of a disjunctive proposition is the truth of at least one disjunct, the necessary and sufficient condition for the falsity of a disjunctive proposition is the truth of neither disjunct. Peter of Spain himself states the falsity conditions in exactly the terms that I have just used. But in so doing he would appear to have abandoned (within a single sentence) his distinction between the more and the less appropriate uses of 'or'. For his more appropriate use is the 'exclusive' use, and a disjunction of propositions connected by the exclusive 'or' is false when both propositions have the same truth value, whether they are both true or both false. Evidently, then, in stating the falsity conditions for disjunctive propositions, Peter of Spain has in mind the inclusive 'or'.

Formally the possibility conditions of a disjunctive proposition are the same as the truth conditions. A disjunctive proposition is possible just if at least one of the disjuncts is possible, and it is impossible if neither disjunct is possible. The impossibility of just one disjunct is insufficient for the impossibility of the disjunction. For if the other disjunct is not impossible it is possible, and if it is possible it might be true. And if it might be true then so might the disjunction, in which case the disjunction is possible. Hence just as a disjunct implies a disjunction of which it is a part, so the possibility of a disjunct implies the possibility of a disjunction of which it is a part.

But the necessity conditions of disjunctive propositions are more complicated. Burley lays down that 'for the necessity of a disjunction it is sufficient that one of its parts be necessary' (*De Puritate*, p. 117). The argument for this position is that a disjunction follows from each of its parts. But from a necessary proposition there follows only another necessary proposition, for otherwise if the conclusion of the inference is only contingent then it might be false in which case what is necessarily true would imply what is false and therefore the inference would be invalid. Consequently if the disjunction has a necessary disjunct the disjunction is itself necessary. But Burley states this as a sufficient, not a necessary condition, because a disjunction might be necessary though neither disjunct is necessary. The general rule is that if two propositions are so related that either is implied by the denial of the other then the disjunction of those two propositions is necessary. As Burley states the matter:

It is sufficient for the necessity of a disjunction that its parts be contradictory, for it is impossible for contradictories to be false simultaneously. Hence it is necessary that one or other contradictory always be true. And so it is necessary that a disjunction composed of contradictories be necessary. (pp. 117–18)

But it should be added that two propositions may, disjoined, form a necessary disjunction even though neither is necessary and neither contradicts the other, for it is possible for two propositions to be so related that either is implied by the denial of the other, even though the two propositions are not contradictory, but instead are subcontrary. Two propositions are subcontrary if they cannot be false together though they can be true together. Thus 'Some man is a logician' and 'Some man is not a logician' are subcontraries. They cannot both be false. If the first of the two is false it follows that no man is a logician, from which, in turn, it follows that some man is not a logician. For if no man is a logician then this (said pointing to a man) is not a logician, in which case some man (for example, this one) is not a logician. And if it is said that where no man exists neither of the subcontrary propositions is true, it should be recalled that a negative proposition with a subject which stands for nothing is true.

A plausible line of argument can be brought to bear on the points just made. It was commonly held that there are no degrees of truth. Or perhaps it should be said, instead, that formal logicians had in general no use for such a concept. There are to be found occasional lapses into modes of expression that suggest that a theory of degrees of truth was held, as for example when Burley asserts that 'The impossible seems to be less true than anything else' (*De Puritate*, p. 61). But in general any proposition that was false was considered to be exactly as false as any other proposition that was false. Indeed, some went further. Paul of Venice asserts:

One proposition is not more true than another, nor more false, nor more possible, nor more impossible, nor more necessary, nor more contingent, but truth, falsity, possibility, and impossibility consist of something indivisible as do rightness and other relations. For just as it is not said that one father is more a father than another father is, or that one equal is more equal than another, so also one thing which is true or necessary is not more true or necessary than another. (*Logica Magna*, 132ra)

Let us attend here to the particular point that truth is without degrees. It might be argued that 'You are or you are not' cannot, therefore, be more true than its first disjunct. But the first disjunct is only contingently true, and hence the disjunction as a whole is only contingently true. And yet it was argued that a disjunction whose disjuncts are mutually contradictory is necessary and not contingent.

But against this argument it has to be said that even if a disjunction is exactly as true as one of its disjuncts and that disjunct is contingently true, it does not follow that the disjunction itself is contingently true. For 'contingent' and 'necessary' are not different calibrations on a scale of truth. A truth is not somehow more true for being necessary than it would be if it were merely contingent. That a proposition is necessary has an immediate implication, at least according to many of our logicians, for its truth value. For if it is necessary it is true. But it is judged necessary in virtue of features it possesses other than its truth value. In particular it is of the essence of a necessary proposition that there is no proposition from which it does not follow, and that every proposition which follows from it is a proposition which follows from any proposition. And it is of the essence of a contingent proposition that it follows from some propositions and does not follow from others. That a necessary and a contingent proposition can both be true is, of course, not in question. The point is, instead, that given that two propositions are both true, questions can then be asked about them in respect of their modal status, and these questions are not about how true the propositions are, about, for example, whether one of them is truer than the other. Paul of Venice compares the relation between the truth and the contingency of a proposition with the relation between the straightness and length of a line. He argues that 'A is exactly as true as B is, and B is a contingent truth. Therefore A is a contingent truth' is invalid in much the same way that this is: 'Line A is exactly as straight as line B, and B is a straight line one foot long. Therefore A is a straight line one foot long' (*Logica Magna*, 132ra).

III. *Conditionality*

We have already noted that the terms 'and' and 'or' have this in common, that each can function as a propositional connective, and also as a connective connecting other than propositions. The same point can be made about the third variety of connective which we shall be investigating, namely, the sign of conditionality. Two such signs were commonly invoked, 'if' and 'unless', the latter being treated as equivalent to 'if not' (see Ockham, *Summa Logicae*, II 31). But most attention was given to 'if', and we shall restrict ourselves to that connective. When 'if' plays the role of forming a categorematic term out of other categorematic terms, it is said to function 'conditionately'. A term thus formed can occur as an extreme in a categorical proposition, as for example in 'Every animal, if it is a brayer, is a donkey', 'Every animal, if Socrates, differs from Plato.' When 'if' plays the role of forming a molecular proposition out of two propositions it is said to function 'conditionally', as it does in 'If an animal is a brayer an animal is a donkey.'

A great deal was written on the question of the rules for determining the relations of valid inference between propositions containing 'if' functioning conditionately and 'if' functioning conditionally. For example, is this argument valid: 'If the Antichrist is a man, the Antichrist is an animal. Therefore the Antichrist, if he is a man, is an animal'? Paul of Venice, who discusses this example among many others, argues that it is not. One reason is that the conclusion is an affirmative categorical proposition, and, as we have already seen, such a proposition implies that there is something for which its subject stands. The subject of the proposition in question is 'The Antichrist, if he is a man'. But the Antichrist, if he is a man, cannot exist unless the Antichrist exists. But the Antichrist does not now exist. Hence, argues Paul of Venice, the conclusion of our sample argument is false. And yet the premiss is true. Therefore the argument is invalid (*Logica Magna*, 134va).

I am not sure that new life can be breathed into the notion of the conditionate 'if', and I would prefer to devote space, instead, to the undoubtedly important concept of 'if' in its conditional role, that is, as a connective which forms molecular propositions out of propositions. The conditional has, then, three parts, the sign of conditionality, and the two propositions which it connects. Of those two propositions the one which immediately follows the 'if' is called the antecedent, and the other proposition is called the consequent. The latter proposition can occur either after the antecedent or before the 'if'. There are, therefore, two basic forms of the conditional proposition, (i) If P, Q, and (ii) Q if P. The antecedent and consequent can both be categorical propositions, and one, or both, can be molecular. That is, to use Burley's terminology explained earlier, a conditional can be either a simple or a composite molecular proposition.

This account of what a conditional proposition is is purely syntactic. In particular nothing has been said about the truth conditions of such a proposition, so there is no suggestion that a proposition is not really conditional if the consequent does not in fact follow from the antecedent. It is sufficient that the proposition consist of two propositions related, in the way already described, by a sign of conditionality. But we should now try to identify the truth conditions of conditional propositions. There was, however, little agreement amongst medieval logicians about the precise formulation of those conditions. Ockham, in line with many others, says simply that a conditional 'is equivalent to an inference, and he will therefore defer discussion of the matter till he reaches the topic of inferences (*Summa Logicae*, II 31). But Ockham is wrong about this. No conditional is equivalent to any inference. The most that can be said is that similar considerations must be brought to bear in determining whether a conditional is true and an inference is valid.

But other logicians did not simply refer their readers to their discussion of the validity conditions of inferences. Paul of Venice lists ten accounts, canvassed at one time or another, of the truth conditions of conditionals (*Logica Magna*, 134va–135ra). Some, for example, argued that a necessary condition for the truth of a conditional is that it should not be possible for the antecedent to be true without the consequent being true. But this was commonly held not to be a necessary condition. And the ground for the rejection was the doctrine that propositions are not timelessly existing entities, but things that exist only while they are being thought or uttered, or while they exist as inscriptions, and therefore they are things which can come into existence and can cease to exist. For it might be said that 'If a man is, an animal is' is true, and yet it is possible for the antecedent to be true without the consequent being true. For 'A man is' might exist at a time when the proposition 'An animal is' does not exist. And at that time 'An animal is', not being anything, is not true either. So at that time the antecedent of the conditional is true and the consequent is not, from which it follows that it must be possible for the antecedent to be true without the consequent being true. And in that case, given that the conditional really is true, it follows that the impossibility of the truth of the antecedent without the truth of the consequent cannot be a necessary condition of the truth of conditionals.

Albert of Saxony reports (*Perutilis Logica*, 19va) that, in the face of this consideration, some revised the earlier account to read: 'For the truth of a conditional it is necessary that the antecedent not be able to be true unless the consequent be true, if each is formed.' We are, then, to assume that antecedent and consequent both exist, and to ask of these two propositions whether the antecedent can be true without the consequent being true. Clearly this manœuvre avoids the earlier difficulty. But another obstacle remains. Consider the conditional 'If no proposition is negative no donkey exists'. This conditional is false since the antecedent and the opposite of the consequent can be true together. That is, 'No proposition is negative' is compatible with 'A donkey exists.' But we are to suppose that the conditional cannot be false unless it is possible for the antecedent to be true and the consequent false. But it is not possible for the antecedent to be true when the antecedent does not exist, so we are to suppose that the antecedent exists. But when it exists it signifies that no proposition is negative. Yet it itself is negative, and hence so long as it exists it is false. And in that case it is not possible for the antecedent to be true without the consequent being true, because it is impossible for the antecedent, when it exists, to be true at all. Therefore the conditional is after all true. Evidently the revised account of the truth conditions of conditionals is not free from difficulties.

In the light of the difficulties raised, Albert offers, and apparently accepts, another account of the truth conditions of conditionals. He states the account as if it is only of the necessary condition, but it seems in fact to be intended as the necessary and sufficient condition: 'It is impossible for things to be in whatever way the antecedent signifies, and yet not to be in the way the consequent signifies, if [each] is formed' (*Perutilis Logica*, 19va). The advantage of this formulation is that in order for things to be in the way a given proposition signifies them to be, the proposition does not itself need then to exist, whereas a proposition has to exist if it is to be true. So things can be in the way signified by 'No proposition is negative' even if there is no such proposition (or only if there is no such proposition), but 'No proposition is negative' cannot be true unless it exists; and, as noted, if it exists it is false.

For all the differences between these, and other, accounts given of the truth conditions of conditionals, one feature they all share is the requirement that conditionality be understood modally. If a given conditional is true then the conjunction of the antecedent and the negation of the consequent is not merely false but impossible. So given the truth of the conditional, either the antecedent is to be denied or, if not, then the consequent must be affirmed, that is, necessarily if the antecedent is to be affirmed the consequent is to be affirmed. It comes, then, as no surprise to find Albert asserting:

For the necessity of a conditional the same thing is required that is required for its truth, and for its impossibility the same thing suffices as is required for its falsity, because every true conditional is necessary and every false one is impossible. (*Perutilis Logica*, 19vb)

The kind of conditionality at issue here, which a later generation of medieval logicians termed 'illative conditionality', corresponds closely to the concept of strict implication, though detailed comparison of the two notions is not appropriate here. But it is at any rate plain that illative conditionality is not the same thing as material implication. For if of two propositions the first materially implies the second, then either the first is false or the second is true, but from the material implication it does not follow that necessarily either the first is false or the second true.

Thus, Paul of Venice asserts:

The argument from an affirmative conditional . . . to a disjunction made up of the contradictory of the antecedent, and the consequent of the same conditional, is a formal inference. This is formal: 'If you are a man you are an animal. Therefore you are not a man or you are an animal.' (*Logica Magna*, 136vb)

His argument is that if P is a condition of Q, then the conjunction of P and not-Q is impossible, in which case the conjunction is to be denied. Therefore one or other of the conjuncts is to be denied. Therefore P is to be denied or not-Q is to be denied. And if not-Q is to be denied Q is to be affirmed. Therefore the disjunction of not-P and Q follows from the conditional affirming that if P then Q.

The preceding discussion gives the main outlines of the concept of conditionality as that concept was expounded by fourteenth-century logicians. As we have seen, the concept closely resembles that of strict implication, and a question naturally arises as to whether medieval logic contains a concept of material implication. There is room for dispute about whether the fourteenth-century texts provide such a concept. But a century later a concept very closely resembling material implication, if not indistinguishable from it, had come to loom large in discussions of conditionality. Promises, and reports to a third person of the content of a promise, are often couched in conditional terms, and for that reason the kind of conditional now in question was called the promissory conditional. Thus, I say to Socrates: 'If you come to me I will give you a horse', and I say to a third person: 'If Socrates comes to me I will give him a horse.' What are the truth conditions of such conditionals?

The great Scottish logician Robert Galbraith discussed this question in his *Quadrupertitum*. He writes:

For the truth of a promissory conditional it is not necessary for it to be impossible for things to be as they are signified by the proposition immediately following the 'if' but not be as they are signified by the proposition mediately following the 'if'. But it is necessary and sufficient that if things are as they are signified by the proposition immediately following the 'if' then they are as they are signified by the mediately following proposition. (*Quad.* 71vb)

For example, 'If Socrates comes to me I will give him a horse' implies neither 'Socrates will come to me' nor 'I will give him a horse.' Neither does it imply that 'Socrates will come to me and I will not give him a horse' is impossible. The necessary and sufficient condition for the truth of the promissory conditional is that if this is true 'Socrates will come to me', then this is true 'I will give him a horse.'

Galbraith asks what form the contradictory of a promissory conditional takes. The answer reveals a good deal about the nature of promissory conditionals. The contradictory of 'If Socrates comes to me I will give him a horse' is, we are told, 'Socrates will come to me and I will not give him a horse.' Now, any proposition is equivalent to the negation of its contradictory. So 'If Socrates comes to me I will give him a horse' is equivalent to 'Not (Socrates will come to me and I will not give him a horse).' But the latter proposition is equivalent to 'Either Socrates will not come to me or I will give him a horse.' Evidently, then, promissory conditionality is truth functional. That is, to know whether such a conditional is true or not it is sufficient to know the truth values of the antecedent and consequent. The conditional is true so long as it is not the case that the antecedent is true and the consequent is false. There is some ground to doubt that Galbraith in fact gave a perfectly unambiguous description of material implication in describing promissory conditionality (see my *The Circle of John Mair*, pp. 147–51). But certainly the concept of promissory conditionality is a good deal closer to that of material implication than is that of illative conditionality. This is made especially plain when Galbraith enquires into the form taken by the contradictory of an illative conditional. He asserts that the contradictory of 'If Socrates comes to me I will give him a horse', where the 'if' is illative, is 'It is possible that Socrates will come to me and I will not give him a horse.' Given the aforementioned principle that a proposition is equivalent to the denial of its negation, it follows that the illative conditional implies 'It is not possible that (Socrates will come to me and I will not give him a horse).' And that last proposition is equivalent to 'Necessarily if Socrates comes to me I will give him a horse.' And we have here a route to the statement quoted earlier from Albert's *Perutilis Logica*: 'Every true conditional is necessary.'

5

Valid Inference

1. *Inference*

Let us say that two propositions are in 'logical sequence' if one follows from the other, and that they are signified to be in logical sequence if one is signified to follow from the other. Two propositions may, of course, falsely be signified to be in logical sequence, and much medieval discussion, some to be noted shortly, stems from this obvious distinction between what is and what is signified to be. But for the present it will be sufficient if certain important terminology for dealing with the relation of logical sequence can be established. Of two propositions signified to be in logical sequence let us reserve the term 'antecedent' to stand for the proposition from which the other is signified to follow. And 'consequent' will stand for the proposition which is signified to follow from the antecedent. We can also say that of two propositions which actually are in logical sequence, whether signified so to be or not, the antecedent and the consequent are, respectively, the proposition from which the other follows and the proposition which follows from the other.

Two propositions related in either of the ways just described were said to stand in the relation of *consequentia*, a term I shall translate as 'inference'. But under the general heading of 'inference' the medieval logicians listed two relations which we should now regard as of logically quite distinct kinds. In fact, despite their practice, it is plain that our logicians also were aware that the two relations are of very different kinds, and their use of the one term *consequentia* should not be allowed to conceal this fact. The two relations in question are that of antecedent to consequent in a conditional, and that of premiss to conclusion in an argument. Correspondingly, two signs of inference were standardly invoked, namely, 'if', as the sign of conditionality, and 'therefore', as the sign that two propositions are related as premiss to conclusion in an argument. Thus 'If P, Q' and 'P. Therefore Q' were both said to have the form of an inference.

However, at least four distinctions were drawn between conditionals and arguments. First, 'if' can connect propositional complexes and 'therefore' cannot. A propositional complex is a unit of speech which is not itself a proposition since its principal verb is not in the indicative mood, though it can be transformed into a proposition by the replacement of the non-indicative verb by its indicative form. Thus, for example, 'A man were to have wings' is a propositional complex corresponding to the proposition 'A man will have wings.' The propositional complex can feature as antecedent in a conditional, but not as a premiss in an argument. 'If a man were to have wings a man would fly' is grammatically sound, but 'A man were to have wings. Therefore a man would fly' just as clearly is not. It was allowed that an argument could have, as a premiss, a conditional which contains two propositional complexes. But that is a different matter. For in such a case the problem is not that of coping with the ungrammaticality of the premiss, but of specifying the truth conditions of the premiss. And that was not considered a serious problem. 'If a man were to have wings a man would fly' is true if it is impossible that things would be as signified by 'A man has wings' without being as signified by 'A man flies.'

The second difference between 'if' and 'therefore' is, like the first, a syntactic one. In a conditional the proposition or propositional complex immediately following the sign of conditionality is the antecedent. But in an argument the proposition immediately following the 'therefore' is the consequent. In an argument the antecedent always precedes the 'therefore'. But in a conditional the consequent can either precede the 'if' or follow the antecedent. Thus, as was observed in Chapter 4 iii, 'If P, Q' and 'Q, if P' both give a form of the conditional. However, the fact that a conditional has these two forms does not mark any serious distinction between it and arguments, for if we take 'since' as a sign of an argument, as it was often said to be, then it can be pointed out that 'Since P, Q' and 'Q, since P' are both grammatically sound forms. We shall, however, retain 'therefore' as the routine mark of inference for the remainder of this book.

Thirdly, the antecedent of a conditional consists of either a single proposition, whether or not molecular, or a single propositional complex. But the antecedent of an argument can be composed of several unconnected propositions, each of which is classed as a premiss. It is not however clear that any important logical truth underlies this fact about the way arguments are set out. Many of our logicians, relying on the distinction between what is explicitly or expressly contained in a proposition, and what is implicitly or virtually contained, often spoke of the premisses of an argument as a conjunction of propositions. Certainly no difference is made to the inferential power of the antecedent of an argument by treating the several premisses as a single conjunction, for even if two premisses are not virtually a conjunction, their conjunction follows directly from the two premisses, and each of the two premisses follows from the conjunction.

The first three differences between conditionals and arguments concern syntactic matters. The fourth does not. It relates to semantic considerations. Truth was in general understood, as we have already seen, in Aristotelian terms, for a proposition was said to be true if things were as the proposition signified them to be. Qualifications and further elaborations of this definition do not here concern us. The point we have to attend to is that logic was regarded as the science that teaches us to speak truly, for by the application of that science we can, starting with true propositions, reach other true propositions. That is how a science, a systematically ordered body of knowledge, is constructed. However brilliantly we reason, it is to no avail if we start from falsity, except where we use the fact that we have reached a false conclusion as itself proof that the starting-point was false and therefore can be transformed into a truth by being negated. But even then the fact that we could start with a false proposition and from it reach a true one does not show that we value falsity as much as we value truth. Quite the contrary, we started with the false proposition in order to prove its falsity, and thereby show our entitlement to replace it by its negation. And that negative proposition could not, on grounds of its truth value, be debarred from a place in a science. But though, being curious creatures, our interest in propositions is really an interest in *true* propositions, and though we use arguments to reach true propositions from other propositions already known to be true, it does not follow that the arguments by which we extend our knowledge themselves have a truth value. Arguments were, indeed, not generally regarded as bearers of truth value, but as bearers of what we might instead call 'validity value' or 'soundness value'. Just as, in respect of the development of science, our interest in propositions is really an interest in true ones, so in respect of the development of science our interest in arguments is really an interest in valid ones. What is wrong with invalid ones is, precisely, that using them we have no guarantee that starting with truth we shall reach truth. The regular ascription of validity or invalidity (or soundness or unsoundness) to arguments, and of truth or falsity to conditional propositions, indicates quite clearly that, though the medieval logicians classed conditionals and arguments under the heading of 'inference', they saw that conditionals and arguments were, in respect of a fundamental principle of classification, in logically quite different categories.

Hereafter I shall use the term 'inference' when I am speaking about that kind of *consequentia* whose distinctive sign is 'therefore', and I shall continue to speak of conditionals when referring to expressions whose distinctive sign is 'if'. Attending then, for the present, to inferences I shall begin by asking how we are to recognize an inference as one. Two views were held on this matter. One was based on purely syntactic considerations. Something is an inference, according to this first view, if it is composed of a set of propositions (perhaps a one-membered set), followed by 'therefore' or one of its synonyms, followed by another proposition. Buridan, however, mentions this view only to dismiss it for his immediate purposes. By 'inference' he evidently means 'sound inference', for he says that by 'antecedent' and 'consequent' he understands propositions of which one follows from another in a sound inference (see *Cons.* a iii). But a piece of speech cannot be an inference unless it has an antecedent and a consequent, and if those two terms are described in the way Buridan has chosen it follows that a piece of speech cannot be an inference unless one part of it actually does follow from the other.

But a question may certainly be raised about whether an inference is an inference only if it is valid. It is of course common enough to meet with an inference which is so bad that it is a travesty of an inference rather than a real one. The fact that it contains a 'therefore' is surely not, we are tempted to think, sufficient to justify its classification as an inference. What, though, of other cases where we do, perhaps only eventually, detect an error in the chain of reasoning? Should such a case not be brought under the heading 'inference'? It might be said that if in fact a given proposition P does not follow from some other given proposition Q, then the relation of P to Q is not an inferential relation. But there is more to inference than a relation between propositions. Inferring is a cognitive act in which, starting with a set of propositions, we draw a conclusion from that set. We infer Q from P. Whether we ought to have reached that conclusion, or ought not, we have all the same inferred Q. If, despite our signifying, by the use of 'therefore', that Q follows from P, it in fact does not follow from P, then we are said to have inferred Q invalidly, and the inference 'P. Therefore Q' is said to be unsound. According to this view, we do not require to know whether Q follows from P to know whether P is the antecedent and Q the consequent in an inference. We need only know whether Q is *signified* to follow from P, and for that it is sufficient to observe that P is connected to Q by a 'therefore'.

The price we have to pay for the adoption of this interpretation of 'inference' is that what we should perhaps prefer to regard as a travesty of an inference has after all to be classified as an inference. But this is a small price to pay, for the alternative is to say that there is no such thing as an invalid inference, only a valid one, and that therefore in order to establish whether something is an inference or not we would first have to establish whether it is valid. Indeed, establishing that it is an inference and establishing that it is valid would be precisely the same thing. But such a line would be very similar to the claim that something should not be called a conditional unless it is true, and that therefore to establish whether something is a conditional it is not enough to observe that it consists of two propositions or propositional complexes connected by 'if'. We have further to establish whether it is true or not. But it was not suggested by any of our logicians that a conditional was a conditional only if it was true. And I shall follow the spirit of this view by accepting the general position that whether or not something is to be called an inference must depend only on certain syntactic considerations and not at all on semantic ones.

Accepting, therefore, that a piece of speech is an inference if it consists of a set (perhaps one-membered) of propositions, followed by 'therefore' or one of its synonyms, followed by another proposition, I shall turn now to the question of the validity conditions of such a piece of speech. It was commonly stated that an inference is valid if it is impossible for the antecedent to be true without the consequent also being true. Or the point can be made in terms of incompatibility: an inference is valid if the truth of the antecedent is incompatible with the falsity of the consequent. And here we must understand two propositions to be incompatible if it is impossible for them to be true together, that is, if the conjunction of them is impossible. But this account of validity meets with precisely the same objection that was levelled at the corresponding account of the truth of a conditional. For we have to remember that propositions were not thought of as timeless entities, but as temporal, coming into existence when they are thought or uttered or inscribed, and going out of existence when the thought or utterance or inscription ceases. And in that case, faced with an inference which we should otherwise wish to accept as valid, we would still have to recognize the possibility that the antecedent might exist at a time when the consequent does not exist. And if the antecedent can ever be true it might be true then, but the consequent would not then exist, and would therefore not then be anything, and therefore would not then be true. And in that case the condition for validity is not met.

We might yield to pressure from this direction and amend our account of validity by requiring that the antecedent cannot be true without the consequent also being true when antecedent and consequent are both formed. We are, then, to ignore what might be the case at those times when one or other of the antecedent and consequent does not exist. But this modification is susceptible to attack from a different direction. Let us consider the inference: 'No proposition is negative. Therefore no donkey runs.' Application of the revised account of validity yields the conclusion that the model inference is valid. But in fact it is invalid, and hence the revised account must be rejected. That it is, on the revised account, valid is easily shown. The antecedent has only to exist to be false, for it is a self-falsifying proposition. And since it is impossible for it, while existing, to be true, it is impossible for it, while existing, to be true without every other proposition which exists at the same time as it also being true, and hence the antecedent cannot, while existing, be true without the consequent, assuming it then exists, also being true.

That the inference is in fact invalid can be shown by invoking the following rule of valid inference: If a given inference is valid then the negation of the antecedent follows from the negation of the consequent. The negation of the consequent of our model inference is 'Not no donkey runs', which is equivalent to 'Some donkey runs.' The negation of the antecedent of that inference is 'Not no proposition is negative', which is equivalent to 'Some proposition is negative'. Hence if the model inference is valid it follows that 'Some proposition is negative' follows from 'Some donkey runs.' And there is no ground whatever for supposing that those latter two propositions stand in the relation of consequent to antecedent in a valid inference.

In the light of considerations such as the one just outlined, a number of logicians adopted a different approach to the question of the validity conditions of inferences. This third approach was characterized by a reluctance to invoke the concepts of truth or falsity. One advantage is the avoidance of embarrassing problems arising from the non-existence of truth-value bearers. The approach was in terms of signification.

According to the view now under consideration, an inference is valid if it is impossible for things to be as signified by the antecedent but not be as signified by the consequent. This account has at least the merit that application of it to the model inference we have been discussing does not force us to the conclusion that the manifestly invalid inference is in fact valid. For it is possible for things to be as signified by the antecedent while not being as signified by the consequent. That things could be as signified by the antecedent would not be disputed by our logicians, for there was not considered to be something peculiar about the class of negative propositions such that at any time at least one of them had to exist. Indeed it was not supposed that there was any proposition of such a nature that it had ever to exist. And at the time, if any, when no negative proposition existed it could be that things were not as signified by 'No donkey runs'. And in that case 'No proposition is negative. Therefore no donkey runs' is not valid.

But even this account of validity was not accepted exactly as formulated above. Buridan, for example, argues that that formulation is too narrow (*Cons.* a iii). The formulation refers to things being as signified by the antecedent and the consequent. But such a formulation leaves out of account the fact that a valid inference may contain past-tensed or future-tensed propositions, and, as Buridan reminds us, a past-tensed proposition is true if things were as the proposition signifies that they were, and a future-tensed proposition is true if things will be as it signifies that they will be. But it is not difficult to see the way we should approach the problem of how to amend the third account in order to deal with this criticism. Thus, for example, let us suppose that the inference which is to be tested for validity consists of a future-tensed antecedent and a future-tensed consequent. As a first stage in the modification of the account of valid inference we could say that that inference is valid if it is impossible that things will be as it is signified by the antecedent that they will be, and yet will not be as it is signified by the consequent that they will be. Inferences which contain past-tensed propositions can be dealt with in a corresponding way. And the fact that an inference may contain propositions of possibility or necessity must also be taken into account. If, for example, the inference to be tested for validity contains an antecedent which is a proposition of necessity and a consequent which is a proposition of possibility, then its validity condition is this: It is impossible that things necessarily are as the antecedent signifies they necessarily are without it being the case that things can be as the consequent signifies they can be.

However, though taking great pains to be precise about the identity of validity conditions, and in consequence being forced to abandon the view that an inference should be called valid merely because it is impossible for the antecedent to be true without the consequent being true, our logicians in fact quite often used this last account of validity conditions, since 'it has counter-examples in few instances' (Buridan *Cons*. a iii). However, some logicians may have spoken of an inference as having an antecedent and a consequent so related that it was impossible for the antecedent to be true without the consequent being true, as a shorthand way of expressing the point that the antecedent and consequent were so related that it was impossible for things to be as signified by the former without being as signified by the latter. Be that as it may, the fact remains that as regards the 'official' account of validity-conditions a consensus formed round the third of the accounts given above.

II. *Kinds of valid inference*

We turn now to certain distinctions which were commonly drawn between kinds of valid inference. And the first of these distinctions is that between inferences which are valid formally and those which are valid materially. A formally valid inference is valid, and every inference equiform to it is also valid (Buridan, *Cons*. a iii). To understand this we have to bear in mind that inferences were thought of as being informed matter. The matter of an inference is every categorematic term in the inference. The form, simply stated, is everything else (see Buridan *Cons*. a v). Connectives, negation signs, signs of quantity ('every', 'some', etc.), and other syncategorematic signs belong to the form. But it is not only syncategorematic terms which should be counted as part of the form. Other aspects of a proposition, which are better thought of as *features* than as terms, are part of the form. Thus the order of terms is part of the form. As noted in Chapter 3, if the position of the predicate term is altered so that instead of being the last term in the proposition it precedes a negation sign which had previously covered it or precedes a universal quantifier which covers the subject, this can have an effect on the truth conditions of the proposition in which that alteration is made. And the fact that the order of the categorematic terms is what it is in relation to the syncategorematic terms is a formal feature of the proposition, though not a feature fully expressed by any syncategorematic term or set of syncategorematic terms in the proposition. And consequently the proposition before the change in order is said to have a different form from the proposition after the change in order. The proposition has been trans*formed*.

A further feature of the form of a proposition is the number of tokens of a given categorematic term. Thus it was held that 'A man is a man' has a different form from 'A man is an animal', simply because the first proposition has two occurrences of a given categorematic term and in the second proposition no categorematic term appears more than once. And two inferences do not have the same form if a categorematic term of a given type appears in more than one proposition in one of the inferences, but there is no corresponding recurrence of a categorematic term of a given type in the other inference. Thus in 'Every man is an animal. Therefore some man is an animal', it is a feature of the form of the inference that the subject in the antecedent is equiform to the subject in the consequent, and that the predicate in the antecedent is equiform to the predicate in the consequent. And hence 'Every man is an animal. Therefore some donkey is an animal' is not of the same form as the preceding model inference. That is, the two inferences are not equiform, and hence the fact that the first is formally valid provides by itself no ground for concluding that the second also is valid. Had 'man' in the subject of the antecedent of the second model inference been replaced by 'donkey', then the situation would have been different, for then the two inferences would have been equiform. And in that case we could have argued that since the first inference is formally valid and the second inference is equiform to the first, the second inference is valid, indeed formally valid, also.

A materially valid inference is simply an inference which is valid though not formally so. That is, other inferences equiform to it are not valid. For example, 'A man runs. Therefore an animal runs' is materially valid. But it is not formally valid, for other inferences of that logical form are not valid, for example, 'A man runs. Therefore a donkey runs.' But there is a question to be asked as to how it comes about that such an inference is valid at all, given that it is not valid in virtue of its form. And one answer that was canvassed was that materially valid inferences are 'reducible' to inferences which are formally valid by the addition of a premiss. For 'A man runs.

Therefore an animal runs' is valid because it is impossible to be a man without being an animal, or because every man is an animal. And if the proposition 'Every man is an animal', which is a necessary proposition, is added to the inference as a premiss, then the inference is transformed from one valid materially into one valid formally. It might, in that case, be said that the original inference was recognized to be valid because the premiss 'Every man is an animal' was, so to say, read into the inference, so that that additional proposition was seen as virtually or implicitly present. And if that is said then perhaps the conclusion to be drawn is that so-called materially valid inferences are formally valid, though enthymematic. An enthymeme is an inference one of whose premisses is unstated. Most of our arguments in ordinary life are enthymemes. Some of the most hardworking premisses are not stated because they are so obviously true, and so obviously at work, that there is no need to state them.

We turn now to a further distinction between inferences. Some are said to be valid simply, and some valid *ut nunc*, that is, as of now, or at present. A simply valid inference is one which, without anything added to it, satisfies the earlier account of validity conditions, namely: It is impossible for things to be as signified by the antecedent and not be as signified by the consequent. On these grounds a materially valid inference can be simply valid even if it is interpreted as an enthymeme which has a necessarily true premiss left unstated. Thus, it is impossible for things to be as signified by 'A man runs' yet not be as signified by 'An animal runs', and hence 'A man runs. Therefore an animal runs' is a simply valid material inference.

Part of the reason for the fact that 'A man runs. Therefore an animal runs' is valid is that 'Every man is an animal' is a necessary truth. That proposition is not just true of the world as at present constituted, but for all time and all space if there exists anything that the term 'man' signifies, then that very same thing is an animal. Put otherwise, wherever and whenever 'A man runs' is said truly, there and then 'An animal runs' would, if said, be true. But there are other inferences which are valid, not because of something which is always and necessarily so, but because of something which is so now. Thus 'Socrates is disputing. Therefore a philosopher is disputing' is valid, not because of something which is always and necessarily so, but because Socrates is a philosopher, which is (we may suppose) now true and is certainly not always true—for when Socrates does not exist he is not then anything and therefore is not then a philosopher. An inference which is valid given the way things are now is said to be valid *ut nunc*.

Inferences valid *ut nunc* have an important feature in common with materially valid inferences, namely, that by the addition of an appropriate premiss they can be 'reduced' to formally valid inferences. The appropriate premiss in the case of the inference valid *ut nunc* is a proposition stating a relevant fact about the way things are now. Thus if we add the premiss 'Socrates is a philosopher' to the premiss 'Socrates is disputing', the conclusion 'A philosopher is disputing' can be drawn as the conclusion of a formally valid inference.

As we have already noted, it was generally held that an inference is valid if it contains as a premiss an impossible proposition. A parallel situation arises in the case of inferences valid *ut nunc*. For it can be shown that an *ut nunc* inference is valid if it contains as a premiss a false proposition, and its validity does not depend in any way on the truth value of the conclusion. Let us take two letters P and Q to be abbreviated propositions. It does not matter what exactly these propositions signify, but let us say that, things being as they are now, P happens to be false. We can now set up the following line of argument:

(1) P   This is false now.
(2) P or Q   From 1, for a disjunction is implied by each disjunct.
(3) Not P   This describes how things are now.
(4) Q   From 2 and 3, for the denial of a disjunct implies the other disjunct.

It follows from this that in an *ut nunc* inference anything whatever can be proved to follow from a proposition false *ut nunc*. And the underlying reason for this is closely allied to the fact that from an impossible proposition anything follows. For let us assume a proposition which is false *ut nunc*. Since it is false its negation is true. And since its negation is true let us assume that negation. In that case we have now assumed a proposition and its negation, and from those two propositions there follows their conjunction. But that conjunction is a contradiction, and a contradiction is a paradigm case of an impossible proposition. And from an impossible proposition anything follows. In particular where a proposition is impossible because it is a contradiction it is easy to show that from it anything whatever follows in a formally valid argument. Thus, just as an *ut nunc* inference which is valid can be transformed into a formally valid inference by the addition of the relevant *ut nunc* true proposition, so where a proposition is known to be *ut nunc* false an inference in which a conclusion is drawn from that false proposition can be transformed into a formally valid inference by the addition of the relevant *ut nunc* true proposition.

Buridan points out that in a sense propositions which are true *ut nunc* are a special group in a wider class of propositions. Starting with our perception of things as they are now (*ut nunc*), we can ask what follows about what else must be the case now (*ut nunc*). But we can address ourselves to the past or future state of things also. Starting from our anticipation of how things will be, we can ask what follows about what else will be the case then (*ut tunc*). And starting from our memory of how things were, we can ask what follows about what else must have been the case then (*ut tunc*). Hence as well as *ut nunc* inferences Buridan speaks of inferences which are valid *ut tunc* ('as of then' as opposed to 'as of now'). Burley, however, in his discussion of inferences valid *ut nunc* gives an account of such inferences which applies equally well to inferences valid *ut nunc* and *ut tunc*. He writes that such an inference 'holds for a determinate time and not always, for example: "Every man runs. Therefore Socrates runs". For this inference does not hold for all time, but only while Socrates is a man' (*De Puritate*, p. 61). According to Burley's account we should have to call the following an inference valid *ut nunc*: 'Socrates will run. Therefore a man will run.' It is not the case that things being as they are now the conclusion follows from the premiss (for Socrates—let us suppose—is not now alive); but given that things will be as they will be, and in particular given that Socrates will be a man, the conclusion follows from the premiss. There is here a difference in terminology between Burley and Buridan, for Buridan would not class the foregoing model inference as valid *ut nunc*. But nothing of logical, as opposed to terminological, significance appears to be at stake in this difference of opinion. For both men would classify the inference as valid, and would do so for the same reason. And each would say that by the addition of the appropriate contingent proposition the inference could be transformed into one which is formally valid.

6

Inference Theory: Medieval and Modern

Modern systems of formal logic and medieval systems proceed in rather different ways, and it will be helpful at this stage in our enquiry to highlight certain of the more important differences. First something should be said about the way modern systems are presented, and on this matter I shall attend to two major approaches. The first is the axiomatic method and the second the method of natural deduction.

A system of formal logic developed axiomatically begins by facing the need to establish a language. So the first step is to stipulate what will count as elements in the language. Thus it might be said that p, q, r, . . . , a, b, c, . . . , F, G, H, . . . , and so on are the elements out of which formulae in the system are to be constructed. Any other elements can occur in the formulae only if they have been introduced subsequently by definitions which employ only elements previously listed. Secondly, rules are given for constructing strings of symbols. Any string which is constructed within the system must be constructed in accordance with those rules. Any string so constructed is a well-formed formula (a *wff*), and any other string must be rejected as ill formed. Thirdly, a set (perhaps one-membered) of formulae is posited as the axiom set. And fourthly, rules are given for transforming formulae into other formulae.

The language thus constructed is, plainly, artificial and an interpretation has to be given. It can, for example, be specified that a, b, c, etc. are to be understood as proper names, or perhaps as symbols which hold a place for a proper name, and that F, G, H etc. are to be understood as predicates, or perhaps as symbols which hold a place for a predicate. The rules of formation are devised to ensure that when the *wff*s are translated in the appropriate way the outcome is a grammatically well-constructed proposition. The formulae in the axiom set are intended to have a certain designated value, say, tautologousness, and the rules of inference are designed to ensure that if a proposition with the designated value is transformed in accordance with the rules of inference, the proposition duly reached also has the designated value.

Systems of natural deduction share with axiomatic systems the first two stages described above. For systems of natural deduction, also, operate with an artificial language, and of course the first requirement in that case is the setting up of principles for generating propositions in the language. But systems of natural deduction do not have axioms. Such systems permit the assumption of any well-formed formula whatever, whether true, contingently or necessarily, or false, contingently or necessarily, and they contain rules of deduction such that if what is assumed is true then what is deduced on the basis of the assumption is also true.

Both kinds of system do, however, have theorems. In an axiomatic system a theorem is any proposition derived, by correct application of the rules of inference, from members of the axiom set. In a system of natural deduction a theorem is any proposition which is reached from a set of assumptions by correct application of the rules of deduction but where, in the course of the deduction, all the assumptions are dropped. It is not necessary to explain here how assumptions can be dropped. It is for the present sufficient to note that both kinds of formal system contain theorems, though not both have axioms.

Other aspects of modern logic could be mentioned here as providing the basis for a contrast with the medieval theory of valid inference. But the foregoing should suffice as such a basis. Let us turn now to the contrast.

The first difference to be noted is visible from a glance at any page of medieval logic. Coming to medieval logic from modern the lack of symbolism is striking. Some symbols were invented. Sometimes letters of the alphabet are used in place of categorematic terms. Sometimes a, i (the first vowels of *affirmo*), and e, o (the vowels in *nego*) are used to indicate universal and particular affirmation, and universal and particular negation respectively. Also, as we shall see in Chapter 8, Section I, certain symbols were invented to do the work of syncategorematic terms. For in late-scholastic logic the first four letters of the alphabet were employed as signs conferring certain kinds of supposition. Thus *b* gives determinate supposition to the immediately following term no matter what kind of supposition the term would have had in the absence of the *b*. But all this amounts to very little indeed compared with the battery of symbols routinely used in modern logic.

The second difference to be noted here is closely related to the first.

Medieval logicians had in general no need to lay down rules of formation. For their investigations were not carried on in an artificial language with which their readers could not be assumed to be familiar, but in Latin, the language of daily discourse for all those who would be reading the textbooks the logicians wrote. If medieval logicians had felt the need to preface their systems with an account of the formation rules of the propositions with which they would be dealing, they would have had to include a textbook of Latin grammar, for it was in such a book that the logic students would find the rules which the logicians followed in constructing the propositions which occurred in their examples of valid inference. The point is that all university students had studied Latin grammar, the first of the seven liberal arts, before reaching university, and did not require lessons in it from logicians.

This is not to say that our logicians had nothing to say about the appropriate grammatical form of propositions which were to appear in valid inferences. They were clear that something had to be said about the acceptable form of a proposition which was to appear in an example of valid inference where, say, rules relating to subjects and predicates were being exemplified. For example, the validity of 'No man runs. Therefore no runner is a man' could not be demonstrated without it first being stated that the premiss is virtually 'No man is a runner'. But this did not amount in the least to providing a list of rules of formation to which all propositions within the system had to conform.

A third difference to be noted is that medieval logic contains no example of a serious attempt to work out an axiomatic system, nor does it give any clear indication of a belief that the axiomatic method is appropriate to logic. Certainly there was available as a model at least one gloriously successful axiomatic system, namely, Euclidean geometry. But its value as a model for logic was simply not recognized.

A fourth major point of difference can now be stated. While there is no merit at all in the suggestion that the logic in the medieval logic textbooks was presented axiomatically, there is merit to understanding that logic as employing techniques of natural deduction. However, modern systems of natural deduction lay down a fixed set of rules of inference. This is not to say that all systems have the same set. They do not, for there are different systems, each appropriate for a different task, and in particular a system designed to deal with one fragment of language can be expected not to have the same set of rules of inference as a system designed to deal with a different fragment. Thus a system which is intended to accommodate propositions which express a relation of identity will require a rule for the introduction, and the elimination, of an identity sign. But all the same, each system has a fixed set of rules of inference.

Medieval logicians, on the other hand, do not appear to have seen merit in presenting a fixed set of rules in their logic. Of course, each set they present is fixed, but there is no doubt that they were fully prepared to supplement their lists with other, many other, rules. Medieval logicians faced with, say, the problem of the validity conditions of syllogisms might remind themselves that a syllogism can contain modal premisses, or a premiss in the past or the future tense. And the standard rules of syllogistic inference are insufficient to permit conclusions drawn from such premisses. So additional rules have to be devised to cope with these new cases. In all this it has to be remembered that when arguing in a natural language there is always the possibility of something unexpected arising for which logicians have not yet produced suitable rules. So the rules of logicians have to be regarded as at best a holding operation until a more suitable set of rules is devised. It can never be known that all rules of valid inference for a given natural language have at last been formulated. The situation is otherwise in the case of artificial languages.

Enough has now been said to indicate that the medieval theory of valid inference was in crucial respects radically different from the modern theory. But before turning to a detailed exposition of rules presented by the medieval logicians, a point of agreement between the medieval and the modern order of doing things should be noted. In our investigation of the way various syncategorematic terms signify, we began by investigating syncategorematic terms which appear characteristically within a categorical proposition, or at least can appear within or as a prefix to a categorical proposition. The terms I have in mind are 'every', 'some', 'no', and 'not'. In the following chapter we turned to a consideration of syncategorematic terms which characteristically connect categorical propositions, so forming molecular propositions out of categoricals. In the earlier phases of medieval logic the theory of inference was treated as a theory applying specifically to propositions in so far as those propositions displayed the form of categoricals. I shall say that rules of valid inference designed to deal with the inferential power of propositions which are specifically categorical are rules for analysed propositions.

But there are also rules of inference which, though applicable to categorical propositions, are applicable independently of the internal structure of those propositions. Instead they apply to categorical propositions merely as propositions, and they apply to molecular propositions merely as molecular. For such rules it is the propositional connectives and the sign of negation which are important, and the quantifiers are of no importance whatever. Rules of the latter kind are rules for what I shall term 'unanalysed propositions'. The expression is not entirely satisfactory since the rules do deal with propositions which are analysed in so far as they are identified as molecular propositions, though they do not deal with propositions which are analysed in so far as they are categoricals containing given quantifiers. The distinction I am making here corresponds to that between inference rules for the predicate calculus and for the propositional calculus. It is well recognized that in the correct order of exposition the propositional calculus comes first, but that this is the correct order was not always obvious. It was not until the fourteenth century that there came to be a reasonably widespread recognition of the importance of expounding the logic of molecular propositions before the logic of categorical propositions. Recognition of its priority appears to have given great impetus to the study of rules of inference for molecular propositions. Certainly in that century great strides were made in that area of logic. Conspicuous amongst the logicians who recognized the priority of propositional logic were Burley, Buridan, and Albert of Saxony. In their writings that part of the theory of valid inference which has special reference to the kind of quantifier expressions propositions contain is discussed only after a preliminary discussion of that part of the theory of valid inference which has special reference to negation signs and to the kinds of connectives that form molecular propositions. I shall begin my examination of individual rules of valid inference by considering rules applicable to unanalysed propositions. I shall use '−' (a minus sign), read as 'It is not the case that' or 'not', to symbolize negation; an ampersand, '&', read as 'and', to symbolize conjunction; 'v' (the initial letter of the Latin *vel* = 'or'), read as 'or', to symbolize disjunction; '→' to symbolise illative conditionality; '↔' to symbolize illative equivalence, that is, mutual illative conditionality; 'pos' to symbolize 'It is possible that'; and 'nec' to symbolize 'It is necessary that'.

7

Validity Conditions and Unanalysed Propositions

1. *Double negation*

Most systems of logic are constructed on the assumption that there are just two truth values, true and false. Other systems, as is well known, are constructed on the assumption that there are more. One logical rule at stake here is that of double negation. Put in semantic terms, this rule states that the truth of a proposition is equivalent to the falsity of its negation. A bivalent system, one assuming that there are just two truth values, accepts this rule. But if there are three values, say, true, false, and undecidable, then the rule is at risk; that the negation of a proposition is false does not imply that the proposition itself is true, for two values remain, not one. It might after all be an undecidable proposition rather than a true one. Medieval logic was not free from disputes about the number of truth values there are. And some logical speculations, prompted by Aristotle's account in *De Interpretatione*, about the sea battle tomorrow, focused on the idea that a third truth value, specially reserved for propositions about future contingent events, may have to be countenanced.

In the past century pressure for a three-valued logic has been thought to arise from the fact that it is possible to construct propositions containing a referring expression which fails to refer. We have noted in an earlier chapter that the medieval logicians faced the problem of the ascription of a truth value to propositions of the kind just described. And their conclusion left intact the fundamental assumption of the bivalence of logic. For they held that if an affirmative proposition contains a subject or a predicate which stands for nothing, then that proposition is false. If no chimera exists then no chimera is anything, and therefore no chimera is white, and in that case the proposition that a chimera is white is false. The point here is that an affirmative subject–predicate proposition was held to make two existential assumptions, namely, that there is something for which the subject stands, and something for which the predicate stands. If either of these existential assumptions is false for a given affirmative proposition then that proposition is false. Buridan lined himself up very firmly with this approach. Nor does he seem tempted by any other consideration to abandon the principle of bivalence. Hence he introduces his list of rules of inference with a statement which proclaims without qualification the principle of bivalence:

Of every contradiction one of the contradictories is true and the other false, and it is impossible for both to be true together or false together. Also, every proposition is true or false, and it is impossible for the same proposition to be true and false at the same time. (*Cons.* a v–vi)

The proposition that every proposition is true or false could be symbolized as: T(P)vF(P). I shall however present it shorn of its semantic garb:

(1) Pv−P.

The proposition that it is impossible for the same proposition to be true and false at the same time could be symbolized as: −pos[T(P)&F(P)]. I shall however present it shorn of its semantic garb:

(2) −pos(P&−P).

The first part of the above quotation from Buridan can be seen to embody the two parts of the rule of double negation. Let us take P and −P as our two contradictory propositions. If P is true then −P is false, and if −P is false then P is true. Expressed syntactically these yield the two rules:

(3) P ∴ −−P.
(4) −−P ∴ P.

Rules 3 and 4 combine to sanction the rule that a proposition is equivalent to itself twice negated, that is:

(5) P ↔ −−P.

This rule is stated most simply by Burley as: 'Two negations make an affirmation' (*De Puritate*, p. 226). He understands this rule to be saying that 'two negations, of which one is so related to the other that it negates the other, make an affirmation, even if the two are entirely related to the same thing.' Burley's exposition is intended to focus on the fact that the rule does not apply to every proposition containing two negation signs, but only to those propositions in which there is what he terms a 'negation of a negation'. For it is not true of all propositions containing two negation signs that the first negates the second; the scope of the first may fall short of the second. Burley gives the example: (i) 'A man, who does not move, does not run' (p. 227). The logically significant feature of this example is that the power of the first negation sign does not extend beyond the relative clause. And since that first negation sign does not cover the second, rule 5 cannot be applied to draw the conclusion that the example is equivalent to (ii) 'A man, who moves, runs.' If there are just two men of whom one does not move and the other moves though he does not run, then (i) is true and (ii) false. The point here is that the non-equivalence of (i) and (ii) is not a reason for rejecting rule 5; it merely shows that (i) does not feature a negation of a negation. In contrast, (iii) 'No man, who moves, does not run' features a negation of a negation, and hence (iii) is equivalent to a purely affirmative proposition, namely, (iv) 'Every man, who moves, runs.'

It is with such examples in mind that Burley refers to the fact that the negation signs must be 'related to the same thing', for where there is a negation of a negation the scope of the second negation is included in the scope of the first. In the extreme case, also noted by Burley, the scope of the two negations is identical, except of course for the fact that the first negation sign includes the second sign, as in (v) 'Not no man is disputing.' By rule 5 example (v) must be equivalent to a purely affirmative proposition. The proposition in question is (vi) 'Some man is disputing.'

The nature of the equivalence relation between a proposition and that proposition doubly negated must be made plain, given that medieval logicians distinguished between two sorts of equivalence, equivalence (a) in inferring, and (b) in signifying. Two propositions are equivalent in inferring if whatever follows from either follows from the other. Two propositions are equivalent in signifying if they have the same signification. Two propositions are equivalent in the second sense if they are subordinate to the same mental proposition. But in that sense a proposition and itself doubly negated are not equivalent, for a certain concept, that of negation, expressed twice in the one proposition is not expressed at all in the other. If a proposition prefaced by two negation signs were equivalent in signifying to that same proposition but lacking the two negative prefixes, then we could not even form a concept of a doubly negated, as opposed to an unnegated, proposition. And in that case we could not conceive the rule of double negation.

II. *Some basic rules of inference*

In this section we shall consider certain rules of inference considered basic by the logicians with whom we are chiefly concerned, and shall introduce other rules they also sanctioned. The order is largely dictated by the order that Buridan adopted in his *Consequentiae*. After laying down the rules, considered in the preceding section, in which he establishes that his logic is bivalent, Buridan turns to a consideration of certain rules of valid inference, and he starts by discussing rules containing the modal operators 'It is possible that' and 'It is necessary that'. The first two rules are as follows: 'From every impossible proposition every other follows, and every necessary proposition follows from every other' (*Cons.* a vi), that is:

(6) $-posP \therefore P \rightarrow Q$.
(7) $necP \therefore Q \rightarrow P$.

Buridan takes these rules to be apparent from a consideration of the definitions of 'antecedent' and 'consequent'. Howsoever an impossible proposition signifies things to be, it is impossible that they be so. And therefore it is impossible that things be as that proposition signifies them to be without also being as any other proposition signifies them to be. Put plainly, given that a certain proposition is impossible, then if its being impossible is not a barrier to its being true then anything can be true. And likewise, howsoever a necessary proposition signifies things to be it is impossible that they not be so. And therefore howsoever any other proposition signifies things to be it is impossible that they be so without also being as the necessary proposition signifies them to be. These two rules correspond to the so-called 'paradoxes of strict implication', but expounded as Buridan expounds them no air of paradox lingers.

Modern logic also has paradoxes of material implication—that from a false proposition any proposition follows, and that a true proposition follows from any proposition. Medieval logic has analogues of these so-called paradoxes. But they are to be found in inferences valid *ut nunc* rather than valid simply. Buridan writes: 'From every false proposition every other proposition follows in an *ut nunc* inference. And every true proposition follows from every other proposition in an *ut nunc* inference.' We saw in the preceding chapter that any conclusion can be drawn from a false proposition in an *ut nunc* inference. That a true proposition follows from any proposition in such an inference can also readily be shown. For either the premiss is true or false. If false, then, as shown earlier, the true proposition follows since any proposition follows. And if the premiss is true, then given that the conclusion also is true, it is clearly impossible that, things being as they are now, the premiss can be true without the conclusion being true, for as things are now the conclusion *is* true.

The next two rules are simply stated: 'From every proposition there follows every other whose contradictory cannot be true together with the first; and from no proposition does there follow another whose contradictory can be true at the same time as the first' (Buridan, *Cons.* a vi); in symbols:

$$(8) \ -\mathrm{pos}(P\&Q) \therefore P \rightarrow -Q.$$
$$(9) \ \mathrm{pos}(P\&Q) \therefore -(P \rightarrow -Q).$$

The arguments for these two rules are as follows: let us assume that P and Q are incompatible—a relation signified by $-\mathrm{pos}(P\&Q)$. As regards rule 8, either P is impossible or it is not. If it is impossible then, in accordance with rule 6, it implies anything, and in that case implies $-Q$. Or P can be true. If it is true then at the same time either Q or $-Q$ is true, in accordance with rule 1. But we have assumed that it is impossible for P and Q to be true together. And hence, if P is true then Q is not. Regarding rule 9, if P and Q are compatible then they can be true at the same time. And in that case the truth of P cannot imply the falsity of Q. Therefore, given the compatibility of P and Q, P does not imply the contradictory of Q.

The reverse of rule 8 was also accepted: 'For a conjunctive proposition to be impossible it is sufficient that its parts be incompatible' (Albert, *Perutilis Logica*, 19rb). One way to expound incompatibility semantically is this: two propositions are incompatible if they cannot be true together. The syntactic version of this account is: two propositions are incompatible if one implies the negation of the other. Let us follow this latter mode of expression and symbolize 'P is incompatible with Q' as $P \rightarrow -Q$. Albert's rule, just quoted, can now be symbolized as:

$$(10) \ P \rightarrow -Q \therefore -\mathrm{pos}(P\&Q).$$

Replacing Q by $-Q$ systematically in rules 8 and 10 we reach:

(11) $-pos(P\&-Q)$ ∴ $P\rightarrow--Q$
(12) $P\rightarrow--Q$ ∴ $-pos(P\&-Q)$.

But rule 5 states that any proposition is equivalent to its double negation, and hence in 11 and 12 $--Q$ is replaceable by Q, yielding:

(13) $-pos(P\&-Q)$ ∴ $P\rightarrow Q$
(14) $P\rightarrow Q$ ∴ $-pos(P\&-Q)$.

It is routine in modern logic to introduce certain logical operators as primitive and to use them to define others which will then be derivative operators. Such an approach to the ordering of operators was not characteristic of medieval logic, though it is clear that it had ample resources to proceed in that way. One move in this direction could have been based on rules 13 and 14. For those rules suggest the possibility of illative conditionality being defined in terms of possibility, conjunction, and negation:

Df. 1: → $\qquad$ $P\rightarrow Q$ =df $-pos(P\&-Q)$.

Replacing Q by P throughout rule 13 we reach:

(15) $-pos(P\&-P)$ ∴ $P\rightarrow P$.

But the premiss in 15 is rule 2. Hence the conclusion of rule 15 can be presented as a rule:

(16) $P\rightarrow P$.

Since rule 16 is the conclusion of 15, the denial of 16 implies the denial of the premiss in 15. The denial of the premiss is, however, equivalent to the affirmation of the possibility of a contradiction. A contradiction is the paradigm case, for medieval as for modern logicians, of an impossibility. Rule 16 is therefore perfectly secure. But medieval logicians were interested in the question of what, if anything, followed from the conditional $P\rightarrow-P$. Evidently it cannot be laid down as a rule that every proposition implies its own negation. But that is not at issue. The question is only whether something can be learned about any given proposition if its negation follows from its affirmation. There are such propositions, in particular, those which are said to 'include opposites'. Burley discusses the curious proposition: (i) 'You know that you are a stone.' The proposition implies (ii) 'You are a stone', since what is known is true. It also implies (iii) 'You are a knower.' But stones are not knowers, and therefore (i) implies (iv) 'You are not a stone.' Since (i) implies the mutually contradictory (ii) and (iv), (i) is said to 'include opposites'. Given (iv), which plainly follows from (i), we can conclude (v) 'You do not know that you are a stone', for given the truth of 'You are not a stone', 'You are a stone' must be false, and what is false cannot be known to be true. Hence (i) implies its own negation. Clearly (i) cannot be true. It is, in medieval jargon, 'virtually contradictory', and hence, howsoever it signifies things to be, they cannot be so. The conclusion to be drawn is that since (i) implies its own negation it must itself be denied. Burley formulates the underlying rule of inference in this way: 'Every proposition which includes opposites implies its own contradictory' (*De Puritate*, p. 70). The kind of proposition which most obviously includes opposites is an explicitly contradictory proposition, one of the form P&−P. But propositions which are implicitly contradictory do not any the less contain opposites, and Burley's rule must apply to them no less than to those which are explicitly contradictory. It therefore applies to the proposition 'Every proposition is true', for if that proposition is prefaced by a negation sign then the latter proposition is true, and if that is true then the first is false, and should be denied. And the proof that it should be denied is precisely that its very affirmation implies its negation. Burley's rule can be symbolized:

(17) P→−P ∴ −P.

Replacing P by −P in (17), and then applying the rule of double negation to the result, we reach:

(18) −P→P ∴ P.

Jan Łukasiewicz titles this rule, or rather the corresponding implication (−P→P)→P, 'the law of Clavius', after a sixteenth-century Jesuit who commented on Euclid's use of the law in his proof of the theorem 'If a^2 is divisible by a prime number n, then a is divisible by n' (see J. Łukasiewicz, *Aristotle's Syllogistic*, pp. 50–1, 80).

We should also bear in mind here the definition, given above, of illative conditionality. P→Q is a shorthand form of −pos(P&−Q). Replacing Q by −P in the definiendum (P→Q) and in the definiens, we reach P→−P as an expression of −pos(P&−−P), that is, of −pos(P&P), which itself is equivalent to −posP. By this means the equivalence of 'P implies its own negation' and 'P is impossible' is easily established. Put otherwise, given that a conditional is true if the antecedent is incompatible with the negation of the consequent, it follows that if P implies −P then P is incompatible with −−P, that is, with P, and hence P must be incompatible with itself. But any proposition incompatible with itself is impossible. So the affirmation P→−P permits the inference of −pos P, and therefore of −P. John Mair discusses the example 'A man is a donkey. Therefore no man is a donkey' (*Introductorium*, 59ᵛ). The point he has in mind here is that 'A man is a donkey' contains opposites, since it implies 'A rational animal is a non-rational animal.' 'A man is a donkey' is therefore incompatible with itself since it affirms of something both that it is rational and that it is non-rational. And such a proposition, since it cannot be truly affirmed, must be denied.

Since we have been employing a concept of illative conditionality defined in terms of the impossibility of a conjunction, certain rules should here be added in clarification of the modal concept in question.

Ockham writes: 'For a [conjunction] to be possible it is necessary that each part be possible' (*Summa Logicae*, II 32). This yields three rules:

(19) pos(P&Q) ∴ posP
(20) pos(P&Q) ∴ posQ
(21) pos(P&Q) ∴ posP & posQ.

However, for the impossibility of a conjunction it is not necessary that each part be impossible, for, as Ockham points out, a conjunction of mutually contradictory contingent propositions is impossible and yet, by definition of 'contingent', each of the parts is possible. Ockham adds: 'For a conjunction to be impossible it is necessary either that one or other of the parts be impossible or that one be incompossible with the other' (*Summa Logicae*, II 32). This may be expressed as:

(22) −pos(P&Q) ∴ −posP v −posQ v P→−Q.

In fact, as Ockham was aware, each of the three disjuncts in the conclusion of rule 22 is by itself sufficient as a premiss of −pos(P&Q). We can therefore add the following three rules:

(23) −posP ∴ −pos(P&Q)
(24) −posQ ∴ −pos(P&Q)
(25) P→−Q ∴ −pos(P&Q).

To complete this section on inferences involving modal operators, certain commonly formulated rules involving modal operators operating on disjunctions will here be listed. Albert writes:

For the possibility of [a disjunctive proposition] it is sufficient that either part be possible for if a disjunctive proposition is possible it can be true but not without either of its parts [being true]. But for the impossibility of a disjunctive proposition it is necessary that each of its parts be impossible, because the disjunction follows from each of its parts. (*Perutilis Logica*, 19va)

There are at least four rules of inference encapsulated in this brief passage:

(26) posP $\therefore$ pos(PvQ)
(27) posQ $\therefore$ pos(PvQ)
(28) $-$pos(PvQ) $\therefore$ $-$posP
(29) $-$pos(PvQ) $\therefore$ $-$posQ.

It is notable that the rules concerning conjunctions and disjunctions are symmetrical. The possibility of a conjunction implies the possibility of each conjunct (rules 19 and 20), and the possibility of a disjunction is implied by the possibility of each disjunct (rules 26 and 27). The impossibility of a conjunction is implied by the impossibility of each conjunct (rules 23 and 24), and the impossibility of a disjunction implies the impossibility of each disjunct. Not surprisingly, the rules concerning the necessity of conjunctions and disjunctions show a like symmetry. The necessity of a conjunction implies the necessity of each conjunct, and the necessity of a disjunction is implied by the necessity of each disjunct. But it is not the case that if a disjunction is necessary one or other of its disjuncts is necessary. Both Ockham and Albert make the point that if the disjuncts are mutually contradictory the disjunction is necessary. And neither of the contradictory propositions need be necessary. Their contradictoriness is, by itself, sufficient to secure the necessity of the disjunction. But there is another relation between the disjuncts which would secure the necessity of the disjunction, namely, subcontrariety. Thus, the disjunction of the propositions 'Some man is disputing' and 'Some man is not disputing' is necessary because the negation of either of those propositions implies the affirmation of the other. Contradictories and subcontraries share the feature that the negation of either proposition implies the affirmation of the other (the law of contradiction adds that either proposition implies the negation of the other). We can therefore add as a further rule:

(30) $-$P$\rightarrow$Q $\therefore$ nec(PvQ).

III. Modus ponens *and* modus tollens

In this section we shall mainly be concerned with a number of rules bearing a more or less close relation to two rules familiar to us under the names *modus ponens* and *modus tollens*. We shall deal first with *modus ponens*.

Ockham writes: 'From a conditional and the antecedent . . . of that conditional the consequent always follows' (*Summa Logicae*, III–1 68). Paul of Venice adds a further detail: 'If of a sound inference the antecedent is true, then the consequent likewise is true. For from something false something true can follow, but from something true nothing except something true follows' (*Logica*, p. 68). An obvious way to symbolize this rule is:

(31) $P \rightarrow Q$, P ∴ Q.

If, therefore, it could be the case that P were true without Q being true, then Q does not follow from P; that is, does not ever follow from P, for here we are dealing with simple, as opposed to *ut nunc* inference. As regards rule 31, if the arrow is interpreted as 'implies *ut nunc*' then $P \rightarrow Q$ is false if, things being as they are now, P is true and Q false.

A stretched version of rule 31 was frequently invoked. For given that a certain inference is valid, then not only does the consequent follow from the antecedent, but additionally (i) whatever follows from the consequent follows from the antecedent. Or, to look at the matter from the opposite direction, (ii) whatever is antecedent to the antecedent is antecedent to the consequent (for i and ii see Burley, *De Puritate*, p. 200). These rules differ only in the order of the premisses. For given a certain conditional $P \rightarrow Q$, anything, say R, which follows from Q follows also from P, and given $Q \rightarrow R$, then anything, say P, which is antecedent to Q is antecedent to R. Thus i and ii can be represented as:

(32) $P \rightarrow Q$, $Q \rightarrow R$ ∴ $P \rightarrow R$.
(33) $Q \rightarrow R$, $P \rightarrow Q$ ∴ $P \rightarrow R$.

Rule 31 is the limiting case of a general rule, and in relation to that general rule the neighbour of rule 31 is 32. The general rule is as follows. Given a series of conditionals so related to each other that, except in the case of the first conditional, the antecedent in each conditional is equiform to the consequent in the immediately preceding conditional, then given the antecedent in the first conditional the consequent in the last can be inferred. Or, to be as precise as our logicians were, from a proposition equiform to the antecedent in the first conditional there follows a proposition equiform to the consequent in the last. This form of argument was known as 'inference from first to last' (*consequentia a primo ad ultimum*), and it was recognized that in a single inference many conditionals could occur as premisses between the first antecedent and the last consequent. We should therefore lay down the following rule:

(34) P→Q, Q→R, R→S ∴ P→S.

But it should be noted that given rule 32, 34 is redundant. For rule 32 can be invoked to infer P→R from the first two premisses in 34, and from P→R plus the third premiss in 34 the conclusion P→S can be drawn, again by rule 32. The point that it was unnecessary to employ more than two conditionals as premisses in order to prove any valid argument that relies on the rule 'from first to last' was known, though not considered of great importance. Much more importance was attached to the requirement that where rule 32 is applied to a pair of conditionals, the consequent in the first conditional and the antecedent in the second should be subordinate to the same mental proposition. That is, physical equiformity is not sufficient to ensure the preservation of truth from premisses to conclusion.

Burley gives a number of examples in illustration of the need to ensure that the consequent in the one conditional and the antecedent in the next one should be not only physically equiform but also subordinate to the same mental proposition. His examples include: (i) 'The more you are ugly the more you adorn yourself. The more you adorn yourself the more you are beautiful. Therefore the more you are ugly the more you are beautiful.' (ii) 'The more you are thirsty the more you drink. The more you drink the less you are thirsty. Therefore the more you are thirsty the less you are thirsty.' Evidently (i) and (ii) are to be understood as containing conditional premisses and conclusions. They could be written so that each begins with 'If', but I shall retain Burley's mode of expression. His point is that both examples commit the fallacy of equivocation by virtue of trading on an ambiguity in 'the more'. This ambiguity is brought out if the examples are rewritten to display more perspicuously the relation between 'the more' in the antecedent and the consequent in each conditional. Let us attend to (ii)—the same considerations apply to (i). (ii) signifies the same thing as (iia) 'By however much more you are thirsty, by that much more you drink. By however much more you drink, by that much more you are less thirsty. Therefore by however much more you are thirsty, by that much you are less thirsty.' And when (ii) is written in this way, rule 32 cannot be applied to it, since (ii) is the wrong shape. That is, the consequent in the first conditional is not equiform to the antecedent in the second conditional. A point of criticism is in order here. It is true, for the reason given by Burley, that what may be called comparative molecular syllogisms are not simply molecular syllogisms with the consequent of one premiss equiform to the antecedent of the other. But this does not supply a rationale for their invalidity—many comparative molecular syllogisms are valid, for example: 'The more people come to the party, the more noise there is. The more noise there is, the madder the neighbours will get. Therefore the more people come to the party, the madder the neighbours will get.' What underlying difference there is between valid and invalid cases is still obscure.

A further apparent counter-example to rule 32, discussed by Burley, involves interesting features not displayed by examples (i) and (ii) above. The example is (iii) 'If I say that you are a donkey I say that you are an animal. If I say that you are an animal I say the truth. Therefore if I say that you are a donkey I say the truth.' For good measure Burley adds that therefore this is the truth, 'You are a donkey' (*De Puritate*, pp. 203–4). The first premiss must, it seems, be accepted. If I say that you are a donkey I say that you are an animal. (I say, in fact, that you are an animal of the donkey kind.) The second premiss also seems acceptable. Given that you are a human being you are an animal, and therefore in saying that you are an animal I say the truth. Arguing from first to last in accordance with rule 32 we reach Burley's conclusion. Now, in (iii) the first premiss is ambiguous. It can be understood to affirm 'If I say "You are a donkey" I say "You are an animal" ', and in that case the premiss is false. And in that case the inference does not proceed from truth to falsity. Or it can be understood to affirm that if I say of you that you are a donkey then I am saying of you that you are (some kind of) an animal. And in that case the premiss is true. But it might then be argued that the conclusion is after all true. That is, if I say that you are a donkey I do say the truth. The truth I say however is not 'You are a donkey', it is instead something implied by 'You are a donkey', namely, that you are an animal. That is, if in saying that you are a donkey I am understood to be saying, amongst other things, that you are an animal, then in so far as I say that you are an animal I am saying the truth. Of course I am not saying nothing but the truth. But it is not stated that I *am* saying nothing but the truth. Clearly the reason why it seems that the conclusion in Burley's sample argument must be false is that we naturally understand it to be saying not only that I say the truth but that the truth I say is 'You are a donkey.' The point emerges plainly if we take the example of the affirmation of a contradiction in which the second conjunct is true. In that case in saying the contradiction I say the second conjunct. And in saying the second conjunct I say the truth. Therefore in saying the contradiction I say the truth. What truth? The truth which forms one principal part of the contradiction. In that case what looks like a counter-example to rule 32 is seen to be no counter-example at all but to be fully and properly sanctioned by that rule.

Further rules related to those just formulated will now be given. 'Whatever follows from the antecedent and the consequent follows from the antecedent by itself' (Burley, *De Puritate*, p. 62); that is:

(35) P→Q, (P&Q)→R ∴ P→R.

The justification of rule 35 is as follows. By rule 16, every proposition implies itself. Therefore if P implies Q it implies itself and Q. (See Ockham, *Summa Logicae*, II 32: 'If part of a conjunction implies the other part then from that first part to the whole conjunction is a sound inference.') Hence, given P→Q, this follows: P→(P&Q). But P→(P&Q) plus the second premiss in 35 yields the conclusion of 35, by rule 32.

'From the antecedent with something added there follows the consequent with the same thing added' (Burley, *De Puritate*, p. 62):

(36) P→Q ∴ (P&R)→(Q&R).

The rule can also be expressed as:

(37) P→Q, P&R ∴ Q&R.

The rule can easily be justified. P follows from P&R. And from P plus the first premiss of 37, Q can be derived. R follows from P&R. Hence both Q and R, and therefore also Q&R, follow from the premisses of 37.

'Whatever follows from the consequent with something added follows from the antecedent with the same thing added' (Burley, *De Puritate*, p. 62); that is:

(38) P→Q, (Q&R)→S ∴ (P&R)→S.

Burley bases his argument for rule 38 on rule 37. From the antecedent with something added there follows the consequent with the same thing added. But (rule 33) whatever follows from the consequent follows from the antecedent. And therefore whatever follows from the consequent with something added follows from the antecedent with the same thing added.

'Whatever is compatible with the antecedent is compatible with the consequent' (Burley, *De Puritate*, p. 63; see Ockham, *Summa Logicae*, III–3 37); that is:

(39) P→Q, pos(P&R) ∴ pos(Q&R).

Suppose that P is true. In that case, given the first premiss of 39, Q is true. And if R, which (by the second premiss) can be true at the same time as P, is in fact true at the same time, it will be true when Q is true. Therefore Q and R can be true together.

'If antecedents are compatible, consequents also are compatible' (Burley, *De Puritate*, p. 63); that is:

(40) P→Q, R→S, pos(P&R) ∴ pos(Q&S).

For let us suppose that P and R are compatible. That is, they can be true at the same time. If they ever are in fact true together, at that time by rule 31 Q must be true and S also. And therefore Q and S are compatible.

We turn now to the rule commonly termed *modus tollens*. Paul of Venice states it as follows: 'From an affirmative conditional along with the contradictory of the consequent, to the contradictory of the antecedent is a sound inference' (*Logica*, p. 80); that is:

(41) P→Q, −Q ∴ −P.

This rule was recognized to stand in close relation to another: 'Of every sound inference, from the contradictory of the consequent there follows the contradictory of the antecedent' (Buridan, *Cons.* a vi), which can be symbolized as:

(42) P→Q ∴ −Q→−P.

And this, in turn, is closely related to: 'Every proposition, formed as an inference, is a sound inference if from the contradictory of a proposition equiform to the consequent there follows the contradictory of a proposition equiform to the antecedent' (Buridan, *Cons.* a vi), which I shall symbolize as:

(43) −Q→−P ∴ P→Q.

My formulations 42 and 43 may not represent Buridan's intentions with complete accuracy. His wording suggests that he may have in mind the justification of the claim that an inference of one kind is valid by reference to the fact that an inference of another kind is valid. For example, the rule I symbolize as 43 should perhaps be taken to say that, given the validity of −Q ∴ −P, it follows that P ∴ Q is also valid. But I shall stay with the formulations 42 and 43.

A proof of 42 was given, which proceeded by assuming the rule unsound and deriving an absurdity from that assumption. Let us assume P→Q and also −(−Q→−P). Now (by rules 12 and 13) −Q→−P is equivalent to −pos(−Q&P), and the denial of that, which we are assuming, is therefore equivalent to −−pos(−Q&P), and hence to pos(−Q&P). By rule 39 whatever is consistent with the antecedent of P→Q is consistent with the consequent. If, then, −Q is consistent with the antecedent of P→Q (which is what our second assumption implies, since −(−Q→−P) implies pos(−Q&P)), then −Q is also consistent with the consequent of P→Q. That is, −Q is consistent with Q. But that is impossible. Given that our two assumptions yield a contradiction, if we retain the first assumption the second must be denied. The denial is −−(−Q→−P), that is, −Q→−P. Q.E.D. The proof of rule 43 proceeds in the same way.

'Whatever follows from the opposite of the antecedent follows from the opposite of the consequent' (Burley, *De Puritate*, p. 65); that is:

(44) P→Q, −P→R ∴ −Q→R.

Burley derives this rule from two other rules, listed above as 32 and 42. The proof is as follows.

  (i) P→Q   = first assumption.
  (ii) −P→R   = second assumption
  (iii) −Q→−P from (i) by rule 42.
  (iv) −Q→R   from (iii) and (ii) by rule 32. Q.E.D.

'Whatever is antecedent to the opposite of a consequent is antecedent to the opposite of the antecedent' (Burley, *De Puritate*, p. 65); that is:

(45) P→Q, R→−Q ∴ R→−P.

The proof of rule 45 is similar to that for rule 44.

(i) P→Q   = first assumption.
(ii) R→−Q   = second assumption.
(iii) −Q→−P   from (i) by rule 42.
(iv) R→−P   from (ii) and (iii) by rule 32. Q.E.D.

Rule 42 is also employed in the proof of a rule commonly invoked, and formulated by Burley as: 'Every proposition which includes opposites implies its own contradictory' (*De Puritate*, p. 70). The simplest case of a proposition which includes opposites is the explicit contradiction. Let us take P&−P as our 'proposition which includes opposites'. Then Burley's rule can be expressed as:

(46) P&−P ∴ −(P&−P).

Let us assume (i) P&−P. A conjunction implies each conjunct. Therefore, (ii) (P&−P)→P, and (iii) (P&−P)→−P. Applying rule 42 to (ii) and (iii) respectively, yields (iv) −P→−(P&−P), and (v) −−P→ −(P&−P). Applying the rule of double negation to (v) yields (vi) P→−(P&−P). Assumption (i) is the conjunction of the antecedents, respectively, of (vi) and (iv). Hence, by application of rule 31, the consequents of (vi) and (iv) can be asserted. But those consequents are equiform with (vii) −(P&−P). And hence, given assumption (i), we can deduce (vii). Q.E.D.

Rule 46 might be thought of as a special case of a rule expressed by Buridan as: 'From every conjunction composed of two mutually contradictory propositions there follows any other proposition, also in a formal inference' (*Cons.* a vii); that is:

(47) P&−P ∴ Q.

And this rule is itself a more specific case of our rule 6, that from an impossible proposition anything follows. Since it is impossible for things to be as signified by P&−P, it is impossible for things to be as signified by P&−P without at the same time being as signified by proposition Q, no matter what Q signifies.

The obverse of rule 47 is the rule that, from any proposition whatever, a disjunction of mutually contradictory propositions follows, that is:

(48) Q ∴ Pv−P.

Since it is impossible for things not to be as signified by Pv−P, then no matter what Q signifies, it is impossible for things to be as Q signifies without also being as Pv−P signifies. From rules 47 and 48 it follows, by the rule 'from first to last', that a conjunction of contradictories implies a disjunction of contradictories.

I shall end this section by considering a small group of rules concerned with conjunction and disjunction. First the rule of so-called 'conjunction elimination': 'From every conjunction there follows each of its parts' (Buridan, *Cons.* c ii). This gives rise to two rules:

(49) P&Q ∴ P.
(50) P&Q ∴ Q.

Ockham, who discusses this rule (*Summa Logicae*, ii 32), adds that the converses of these rules do not work, except sometimes for 'material' reasons. It is possible that what he has in mind here is that an inference such as 'Socrates is a man. Therefore Socrates is a man and Socrates is an animal' is valid, though not formally, because of the relation between the concepts of 'man' and 'animal'. But if this is Ockham's position it is incorrect. An argument of the form 'P. Therefore P&Q' may be valid for formal reasons. For example, where the first proposition in a conjunction is a contradiction, then the conjunction follows from that contradiction, and does so for formal and not material reasons. For an inference whose premiss is a contradiction is formally valid. Propositions can be placed on a line whose termini mark points of greatest strength and greatest weakness. Let us say that of two propositions one is formally stronger than the other if for formal reasons it implies the other but is not for formal reasons implied by the other. The principle at issue here can now be expressed as follows: Given a conjunction of which one conjunct is formally stronger than the other, then not only does each conjunct follow formally from the conjunction but the conjunction itself follows formally from the formally stronger of the two conjuncts. As regards a conjunction of which one principal part is a contradiction, the contradiction formally implies the other part, since a contradiction formally implies anything whatever—it has the greatest strength that any proposition can have. Hence not only does each conjunct follow from that conjunction, but the conjunction itself follows from the part which is a contradiction.

In fact I have not stated the only circumstance in which it is permissible on formal grounds to deduce a conjunction from one of its conjuncts. Suppose that two propositions, P and Q, for formal reasons imply each other. In that case, of course, on a given line calibrated in terms of formal strenth P and Q must occupy the same point. Where P and Q are thus related, their conjunction follows formally from each of P and Q. To take the simplest kind of case, if two propositions are mutually equiform then a proposition equiform with either of them implies their conjunction. Thus P&P follows from P. To state the rule more generally than I have done so far, if two propositions, P and Q, are so related that P is not less strong than Q, formally speaking, then the conjunction of the two propositions follows formally from P.

This discussion suggests that one further rule can now be stated, specifying the condition in which the 'fallacy of the consequent' is not committed when arguing from a conjunct to a conjunction:

(51) P→Q, P ∴ P&Q.

Ockham was familiar with the rule just stated. He writes: 'If one part of a conjunctive proposition implies the other part then from that part to the whole conjunctive proposition is a sound inference' (*Summa Logicae*, II 32).

Let us turn now to the rule of 'disjunction introduction'. Albert writes: 'From each part of an affirmative disjunctive proposition to the affirmative disjunctive proposition of which it is a part, is a sound inference' (*Perutilis Logica*, 19ra). Buridan states the matter rather differently: 'From every proposition there follows itself disjoined from any proposition' (*Cons.* c ii). This gives rise to two rules:

(52) P ∴ PvQ.
(53) Q ∴ PvQ.

Ockham, also, states these rules. He adds: 'The reverse inference involves the fallacy of the consequent, though sometimes there is some special obstacle to that fallacy' (*Summa Logicae*, II 33). The fallacy of the consequent 'arises because people suppose the relation of inference to be reciprocal. For whenever, suppose *this* is, *that* necessarily is, they suppose that if the latter is, the former necessarily is' (Aristotle, *Soph. Elenchi*, 167b1 ff.). The point here is that the fact that a given argument, say one from a disjunct to the disjunction, is valid, does not by itself justify the claim that the reverse argument, say from the disjunction to a disjunct, is also valid. The reverse argument might in fact be valid, but not because the original one is. Ockham claims that in the case of rules 52 and 53 the reverse argument is indeed sometimes valid, that there is sometimes 'some special obstacle to the fallacy of the consequent'. Consideration of our discussion following rules 49 and 50 reveals what the special obstacle is. Let us suppose that P is, in the sense defined above, formally stronger than Q. In that case Q follows formally from the disjunction of P and Q. Thus, for example a contingent proposition follows formally from any disjunction in which that contingent proposition is disjoined from an explicit contradiction. For an explicit contradiction is formally stronger than any contingent proposition. And likewise, a formally necessary proposition follows from any disjunction in which that necessary proposition is disjoined from a contingent proposition. For every contingent proposition is stronger than any necessary proposition.

But again, it should be said that the foregoing conditions in which a disjunct follows formally from a disjunction are not the only conditions. It is sufficient that of two propositions each is precisely as strong as the other, formally speaking. Thus, P follows from PvP, and from Pv−−P. Therefore, to state the rule more generally than I have done so far, if two propositions, P and Q, are so related that P is not less strong than Q, formally speaking, then Q follows formally from the disjunction of P and Q.

We can now state a further rule specifying the 'special obstacle' which allows us to argue from a disjunction to a disjunct without committing the 'fallacy of the consequent':

(54) P→Q, PvQ ∴ Q

We turn to a further rule involving disjunction. Buridan invokes the concept of a 'sufficient division' and says of it that if one of its heads of division is denied the other should be inferred. In illustration he offers the inference: 'Every A is B or every A is C. And an A is not B. Therefore every A is C' (*Cons.* c ii). Evidently, then, Buridan's inference can be seen as illustrating the rule formulated by Ockham as: 'From a disjunctive proposition, along with the negation of one of its parts, to the other part, is a sound inference' (*Summa Logicae*, II 33); that is:

(55) PvQ, −P ∴ Q.
(56) PvQ, −Q ∴ P.

Ockham's example is however, as it stands, less helpful than Buridan's. For Ockham writes: 'Socrates is a man or a donkey. Socrates is not a donkey. Therefore Socrates is a man.' But the first premiss is not in fact a disjunctive proposition and in that case the rule is not applicable to it. The point is that the disjoint 'or' in the first premiss is to be understood divisively, so that the premiss should be taken as equivalent to the disjunctive proposition 'Socrates is a man or Socrates is a donkey.' And when the first premiss is replaced by its disjunctive equivalent then the rule can indeed be applied to the two premisses to yield the conclusion Ockham specifies.

A set of rules, commonly known today as De Morgan's laws, after the nineteenth-century mathematician and logician Augustus De Morgan, was part of the repertoire of all the medieval logicians with whom I have been concerned. Albert of Saxony writes:

The contradictory of a conjunctive proposition is a disjunctive proposition composed of parts which are the contradictories of the parts of the conjunctive proposition. . . . The contradictory of an affirmative disjunctive proposition is a conjunctive proposition composed of parts which are the contradictories of the parts of the disjunctive proposition. (*Perutilis Logica*, 19[rb])

Two propositions are contradictories if each implies the negation of the other and the negation of each implies the other. The above two rules, therefore, yield the following four rules:

(57) $P\&Q \therefore -(-Pv-Q)$
(58) $PvQ \therefore -(-P\&-Q)$
(59) $-(P\&Q) \therefore -Pv-Q$
(60) $-(PvQ) \therefore -P\&-Q$

The validity of 58 and 60 is guaranteed by the validity of 57 and of 59 respectively. Proof:

(57a) $--(-Pv-Q) \therefore -(P\&Q)$

is valid given 57, since if a given inference is sound, then from the negation of the conclusion there follows the negation of the premiss.

(57b) $-Pv-Q \therefore -(P\&Q)$

is valid given 57a, by application of the rule of double negation.

(57c) $--Pv--Q \therefore -(-P\&-Q)$

is valid given 57b, replacing P by $-P$ and Q by $-Q$ systematically. 58 is valid given 57c by application of the rule of double negation. Q.E.D.

60 is derivable from 59 by the same means.

It can also be shown that each of these rules is valid if reversed. For example, if in 60 P is replaced by −P and Q by −Q systematically, and the rule of double negation is then applied, the result is the converse of 57. By similar means the converse of 58 is derived from 59, of 59 from 58, and of 60 from 57.

It follows from 57, or rather from 57 expressed as a mutual inference, that the conjunction sign need not be treated as a primitive sign, but can instead be defined in terms of disjunction and negation. And likewise it follows from 58 expressed as a mutual inference that the disjunction sign can be defined in terms of conjunction and negation. But our logicians did not give such definitions. It was sufficient for their purposes that they were aware of the logical relations between the concepts of conjunction and disjunction. No goal, worthwhile in relation to their brief, would have been secured by defining '&' as P&Q =df −(−Pv−Q), or by defining 'v' in a parallel way. It is not that medieval logicians were loath to offer definitions. They gave a great many. But definition had a purpose, namely to clarify the comparatively obscure. Conjunction and disjunction were simply not obscure enough to merit definition, and certainly neither could reasonably be claimed to be more obscure than the other.

On the basis of 59 let us argue as follows:

(i)   −(P&Q) = first assumption
(ii) P   = second assumption
(iii) −Pv−Q from (i) by rule 59
(iv) −−P   from (ii) by rule 3
(v)   −Q   from (iii) and (iv) by rule 55.

Therefore (v) is deducible from (i) and (ii). This inference can be set out as follows:

(61)   −(P&Q), P ∴ −Q.

It is easy to show that the following also is valid:

(62)   −(P&Q), Q ∴ −P.

The rule here is: 'From a negated conjunction, along with one of the conjuncts, to the negation of the other conjunct, is a valid inference' (see Andreas Kesler, *De Consequentia Tractatus Logicus*, 141).

Amongst the many modes of valid inference listed by the medieval logicians there are four, forming a neat group, which have now been examined in this chapter. The four, with their Latin names, are as follows:

(M1) P→Q, P ∴ Q = *modus ponendo ponens*, that is, while affirming (the antecedent), affirming (the consequent).

(M2) P→Q, −Q ∴ −P = *modus tollendo tollens*, that is, while denying (the consequent), denying (the antecedent).

(M3) PvQ, −P ∴ Q = *modus tollendo ponens*, that is, while denying (one disjunct), affirming (the other disjunct).

(M4) −(P&Q), P ∴ −Q = *modus ponendo tollens*, that is, while affirming (one conjunct), denying (the other conjunct).

I shall complete this section by establishing a rule which plays a part in syllogistic theory.

   (i) (P&Q)→R   = first assumption
  (ii) −R&P   = second assumption
 (iii) −R→−(P&Q) from (i) by rule 42
 (iv) −R   from (ii) by rule 49
  (v) P   from (ii) by rule 50
 (vi) −(P&Q)   from (iv), (iii), by rule 31
(vii) −Pv−Q   from (vi) by rule 59
(viii) −−P   from (v) by rule 3
 (ix) −Q   from (vii), (viii), by rule 55
  (x) (−R&P)→−Q from (ii), (ix), on first assumption.

Therefore from first to last, that is, from (i) to (x):

(63) (P&Q)→R ∴ (−R&P)→−Q

By a similar line of reasoning:

(64) (P&Q)→R ∴ (P&−R)→−Q
(65) (P&Q)→R ∴ (−R&Q)→−P
(66) (P&Q)→R ∴ (Q&−R)→−P

8

Validity Conditions and
Analysed Propositions

1. *The square of opposition*

In the previous chapter we attended to rules of valid inference for unanalysed propositions. That is, although propositions are either categorical or composed of categoricals, the distinctive features of categorical propositions, in particular, their subject–predicate structure, and their universality, particularity, or singularity, were not relevant to the rules. For example, the rule sanctioning the move from a proposition to the negation of its negation holds for all categorical propositions whether universal or otherwise, and holds also for all non-categorical propositions. In this chapter attention will be paid to the inferential power of categorical propositions where the structure of those propositions is taken into account.

At the heart of the medieval theory of valid inference for analysed propositions lies an account of three ways in which two categorical propositions with the same categorematic terms may be related to each other. They may be related by opposition, equipollence, or conversion. Propositions related by opposition or equipollence have the same categorematic terms in the same order; where the relation is that of conversion the order is not the same. Equipollence is a relation of equivalence between two propositions structurally related to each other in a certain quite specific way. Opposition is not a relation of equivalence. These are the main differences between these kinds of relation. We are concerned here with the relations because they all give rise to rules of inference. We shall start, where most medieval discussions in this area started, with the notion of opposition.

Perhaps the best-known notion of medieval logic is that of the square of opposition. But medieval logicians liked such squares and drew a considerable variety of them. We shall start by considering the simplest. At different places in the course of this book, aspects of the simplest square of opposition have been invoked. But now we shall draw the various threads together. Let us for the time being ignore categorical propositions whose subject is a proper name and focus instead on categorical propositions which are either universal or particular. Such propositions can be either affirmative or negative. We have to deal, then, with four kinds of proposition. Using a, e, i, and o as signs of universal affirmation, universal negation, particular affirmation and particular negation, we can symbolize the four kinds of proposition as AaB, AeB, AiB, and AoB. There is no obvious sense in which each proposition of these four is opposed to all the others, but there is a reasonably obvious sense in which AaB is opposed to AeB and AoB, and in which AiB is opposed to AeB and AoB, namely, in the sense that AaB and AiB are related to AeB and AoB as affirmation to negation. The relation between AaB and AiB, and also the relation between AeB and AoB, were called relations of opposition because of their place in the square of opposition, rather than because of any obvious sense in which those propositions were opposed. It might be said that AaB and AiB are opposed in that the first is universal and the second particular, but if so then any difference might have to be called an opposition, and then the concept of opposition would lose its point. We shall start by considering the relation between AaB and AeB.

Two universal propositions equiform except that one is affirmative and the other negative are related as contraries. Peter of Spain writes: 'The law of contraries is such that if one [proposition] is true, the other is false, and not vice versa' (*Tractatus*, p. 7). Peter expounds the relation of contrariety in semantic terms, but a syntactic account can be drawn from the semantic version. Peter's law thus yields three rules:

(1) AaB ∴ −(AeB)
(2) AeB ∴ −(AaB)
(3) −pos(AaB & AeB).

The underlying logical relation between contrary propositions is that expressed in one of the De Morgan rules discussed in the preceding chapter. Rule 60 sanctions the move from the denial of a disjunction to the affirmation of a conjunction whose parts are the contradictories of the parts of the disjunction. And it was stated that the reverse inference also holds. In the light of this equivalence in inferential power, we can argue as follows:

(i) −(PvQ)&−(RvS)   = first assumption
(ii) −(PvQ)   from (i) by rule 49 (ch. 7)

(iii) $-(RvS)$ from (i) by rule 50 (ch. 7)
(iv) $-P\&-Q$ from (ii) by rule 60 (ch. 7)
(v) $-R\&-S$ from (iii) by rule 60 (ch. 7)
(vi) $(-P\&-Q)\&(-R\&-S)$ from (iv) and (v), since from two
                                          propositions to their conjunction is
                                          a valid inference.

Let us now make certain replacements in (vi). P is to be replaced by $A^1=B^1$. Since in (vi) P is negated, $A^1=B^1$ will have to be negated also. That negation can be expressed as $A^1\neq B^1$. So instead of $-P$ we write $A^1\neq B^1$. Likewise let us replace Q by $A^1=B^2$ (which will be duly negated and expressed as $A^1\neq B^2$). We shall replace R by $A^2=B^1$, and S by $A^2=B^2$, and negate them likewise. The result of these replacements in (vi) is:

(vii) $(A^1\neq B^1\ \&\ A^1\neq B^2)\ \&\ (A^2\neq B^1\ \&\ A^2\neq B^2)$.

Now, in AeB the subject and predicate both have distributive supposition, and hence descent is to be made under each of them to a conjunction of singular propositions. Since they have the same kind of supposition the order of descent is immaterial. Let us, therefore, assume that there are just two things, A^1 and A^2, which are A, and just two things, B^1 and B^2, which are B, and we shall descend first under A and then under B. The conjunction of singular propositions reached by this procedure is (vii).

We turn now to AaB, and argue as follows:

(viii) $(PvQ)\&(RvS)$ second assumption
(ix) PvQ from (viii) by rule 49 (ch. 7)
(x) RvS from (viii) by rule 50 (ch. 7)

In (ix) let us make the same replacements that were made for step (vii):

(xi) $(A^1=B^1)\ v\ (A^1=B^2)$ from (ix), replacing P by $A^1=B^1$, Q
                                   by $A^1=B^2$.

But if A^1 is identical with B^1 or is identical with B^2, then it is identical with B^1vB^2. Therefore:

(xii) $A^1=B^1vB^2$ from (xi)
(xiii) $(A^2=B^1)\ v\ (A^2=B^2)$ from (x), replacing R by $A^2=B^1$, S by
                                   $A^2=B^2$

But if A^2 is identical with B^1 or is identical with B^2, then it is identical with B^1vB^2. Therefore:

(xiv) $A^2 = B^1vB^2$ from (xiii)

(xv) $(A^1 = B^1vB^2)$ & $(A^2 = B^1vB^2)$ from (xii) and (xiv), since from two propositions to their conjunction is a valid inference.

Now, in AaB the subject has distributive supposition and the predicate merely confused supposition. Descent should therefore be made first to a conjunction of singular propositions under A, and then to a disjunction of singular terms under B. Let our domain, once again, be A^1, A^2, B^1, B^2. The two stages of descent take us to (xv). And hence, for the domain just described, (xv) is equivalent to:

(xvi) AaB

The point to note here is the relation between (i) and (viii). Both are conjunctions, and the conjuncts affirmed in (viii) are negated in (i). Clearly, of two such conjunctions if one is true the other is false, and it does not follow from one being false that the other is true. That is, the law of contraries applies to them. What has just been demonstrated is that it is because the law of contraries applies to two such conjunctions that it applies to AaB and AeB.

We turn now to the second of the relations of opposition represented in the square of opposition, namely, contradiction. Peter of Spain writes: 'The law of contradictories is such that if one [proposition] is true the other is false, and vice versa' (*Tractatus* p. 7). This relation holds between two propositions which differ in both quantity and quality. Thus AaB and AoB are contradictories, as are AeB and AiB. Since the truth of each member of the pair implies the falsity of the other, and the falsity of each implies the truth of the other, each member of the pair is equivalent to the negation of the other. We shall however, for the present, set out the inferences as one-way:

(4) AaB ∴ −(AoB)

(5) AeB ∴ −(AiB)

(6) AiB ∴ −(AeB)

(7) AoB ∴ −(AaB)

(8) −(AoB) ∴ AaB

(9) −(AiB) ∴ AeB

(10) −(AeB) ∴ AiB

(11) −(AaB) ∴ AoB

(7) holds if (4) does, in accordance with the rule that if an inference is valid then from the negation of the conclusion to the negation of the premiss is a valid inference. That yields $--$(AoB) as the premiss of $-$(AaB). And the law of double negation can then be applied to that premiss, thus yielding (7). In much the same way, it can be argued that (6) holds if (5) does. Likewise (11) holds if (8) does, and (10) if (9) does.

The logical basis of the contradictoriness of AaB and AoB can be displayed as follows:

  (i) (PvQ)&(RvS)   = first assumption
 (ii) AaB   from (i); see steps (viii)–(xv) above,
                                 and the paragraph following (xv).
(iii) $-$(PvQ)v$-$(RvS)   = second assumption
 (iv) ($-$P&$-$Q)v($-$R&$-$S)   from (iii) by replacing each
                                 disjunction in (iii) by its De Morgan
                                 equivalent (see rule 60 (ch. 7)).

Replacing P by $A^1=B^1$, Q by $A^1=B^2$, R by $A^2=B^1$, and S by $A^2=B^2$, in (iv), and expressing the negation of those identities by the sign of non-identity ($\neq$), we reach:

  (v) $(A^1\neq B^1$ & $A^1\neq B^2)$ v $(A^2\neq B^1$ & $A^2\neq B^2)$.

Given that there are just two things, A^1 and A^2, which are A, and just two things, B^1 and B^2, which are B, descent to singulars under AoB takes us first to: A^1 is not B or A^2 is not B. And the second stage of descent takes us to (v). Thus, for the domain just described (v) is equivalent to:

  (vi) AoB.

The point to note here is the relation between (i) and (iii). It is that between a conjunction of propositions and a disjunction whose principal parts are the negations of the principal parts of the conjunction. (i) and (iii), being so related, cannot both be true and cannot both be false. That is, the law of contradictories applies to them. What has just been demonstrated is that it is because the law of contradictories applies to (i) and (iii) that it also applies to AaB and AoB. By a similar line of reasoning it can be shown that it is because the law of contradictories applies to (PvQ)v(RvS) and $-$(PvQ)& $-$ (RvS), that it also applies to AiB and AeB.

The third variety of opposition is that of subcontrariety. Peter of

Spain writes: 'The law of subcontrarieties is such that if one [proposition] is false the other is true, and not vice versa' (*Tractatus*, p. 7). This yields three inferences:

(12) $-(AiB) \therefore AoB$
(13) $-(AoB) \therefore AiB$
(14) pos(AiB & AoB)

(12) and (13) each hold if the other does. For given (12), from the negation of its conclusion there follows the negation of its premiss. And by applying the rule of double negation to the resulting conclusion we reach (13). In the same way (12) can be derived from (13).

The fact that AiB and AoB can be true together might call in question the propriety of speaking of the relation of subcontrariety as a form of opposition. But there is an opposition, though a syntactic rather than a semantic one. It lies, as was stated earlier, in the fact that one is affirmative and the other is exactly like the first except for containing a negation sign.

We turn now to the fourth and last variety of opposition, that of subalternation. Peter of Spain writes: 'The law of subalternates is such that if a universal is true a particular is true, and not vice versa. For a universal can be false while its particular is true. And if a particular is false its universal is false, and not vice versa' (*Tractatus*, p. 7). This yields two rules of inference:

(15) AaB $\therefore$ AiB
(16) AeB $\therefore$ AoB

(15) is derivable from the rule (itself readily derivable from rules 49 and 52, ch. 7) that from a conjunction to a disjunction whose parts are the same as those of the conjunction is a valid inference. The proof is as follows:

(i) AaB = assumption

For the domain we have been assuming, (i) is equivalent to:

(ii) $(A^1 = B^1 v A^1 = B^2) \& (A^2 = B^1 v A^2 = B^2)$
(iii) $(A^1 = B^1 v A^1 = B^2) v (A^2 = B^1 v A^2 = B^2)$ from (ii) by the rule that from a conjunction to a disjunction with the same parts is a valid inference.

For the domain we have been assuming, (iii) is equivalent to:

(iv) AiB

Therefore from first to last: AaB ∴ AiB   = 15   Q.E.D.

(16) can be established by similar means.

A later generation of logicians did not tie the notion of subalternation exclusively to a relation between a universal and a particular proposition. Thus George Lokert asserts: 'An affirmative disjunctive proposition is subalternate to an affirmative conjunctive proposition composed of the same parts' (*De Opp.* 35[ra–b]). Such an extension of the notion of subalternation leads to the notion being indistinguishable from that of one-way valid inference.

Rule 15 reminds us of the 'existential import' of universal affirmative propositions as these were understood by medieval logicians. A universal affirmative proposition, say 'Every whale is a mammal', would be said by most modern logicians to have a form more perspicuously represented by 'For every x, if x is a whale then x is a mammal', that is, it has the form $(x)(Wx{\rightarrow}Mx)$. And as so understood, the proposition could be true though no whale existed. But on the modern interpretation of particular affirmative propositions, say 'Some whale is a mammal', the logical form of this proposition is more perspicuously represented by 'For some x, x is a whale and x is a mammal', that is, it has the form $(Ex)(Wx\&Mx)$. And on this interpretation the proposition does imply that a whale exists. On the modern view, therefore, the universal affirmative proposition in one respect makes a stronger claim, and in another a weaker, than the particular affirmative. For the universal affirmative makes a claim about everything, but without implying the existence of anything, whereas the particular affirmative both makes a claim about something, and also implies the existence of that thing. For this reason the inference from the universal affirmative to the particular is invalid, on the modern interpretation. But as we have seen, medieval logicians invoked rules of descent, rules which were regarded expressly as rules of valid inference. Thus every affirmative categorical proposition, whether universal or particular, implies at least one singular proposition affirming that something signified by the subject is identical with something signified by the predicate. Given AaB, it follows that there is something which is both A and B. AaB, therefore, has the existential import which it must have if AiB is to be deducible from it.

A closely related point can be made about negative categorical propositions. 'No A is B' has two mutually equivalent modern interpretations, namely 'It is not the case that for some x, x is A and x is B' and 'For every x, if x is A then x is not B', in symbols respectively:

(i) $-(Ex)(Ax\&Bx)$

(ii) $(x)(Ax\rightarrow -Bx)$

'Some A is not B' is interpreted as 'For some x, x is A and x is not B', in symbols:

(iii) $(Ex)(Ax\&-Bx)$

From (iii) there follows

(iv) $(Ex)Ax$

But (iv) does not follow from (i). That it does not is perhaps clearer in the light of the consideration that (i) and (ii) are equivalent. All that (ii) says is that if anything is A it is B. And this carries no implication as to whether there is or is not something which is A. But though (iii) is not subalternate to (i), AoB is subalternate to AeB. This is possible because neither AeB nor AoB implies that the subject has a significate. But each implies that if the subject has significates then at least one of those significates is not also a significate of the predicate. The ground principle here is that a negative categorical proposition is true if either of its extremes has no significate. It is easy to see this point as regards universal negative propositions. No A is B if there is no A, for if there is no A then there is no A to be anything, and therefore none to be B. As regards particular negative propositions, we should bear in mind here rules 7 and 11 above, according to which $-(AaB)$ and AoB follow from each other. If there is nothing which is A then it is not the case that every A is B. For, as was just observed, if nothing is A, *no* A is B. That is, from 'There is no A' $-(AaB)$ follows, and therefore its equivalent, namely AoB, follows also.

Thus, although there are two basic principles of division for a, e, i, and o propositions, namely quantity (universal or particular) and quality (affirmative or negative), as regards ontological significance it might seem that the more basic division is that into affirmation and negation, because that principle divides propositions according as they do or do not imply the existence of significates of their terms. But that point should be held lightly, for the division into universal and particular also has existential implications. AaB and AeB both imply a non-existence, namely of an A which is not B, and of an A which is B, respectively. And AiB and AoB do not imply the non-existence of an A which is not B, and of an A which is B, respectively.

Of the sets of rules concerning contrariety, contradiction, subcontrariety, and subalternation, none of these seems to have logical priority over the others. That is, there seems no good logical reason why certain of these sets should be treated as primary and the rest derivative. Certainly, three of the sets can be derived from the others. Let us begin with the rules of subalternation. These can be derived via the rules of contrariety and contradiction. For example:

    (i)   AaB   = assumption
    (ii) −(AeB) from (i) by rule 1
    (iii) AiB   from (ii) by rule 10
Therefore from first to last: AaB ∴ AiB   (= rule 15).

Likewise the rules of subcontrariety can be derived via the rules of contradiction and of subalternation. For example:

    (i) −(AoB) = assumption
    (ii) AaB   from (i) by rule 8
    (iii) AiB   from (ii) by rule 15
Therefore from first to last: −(AoB) ∴ AiB   (= rule 13).

Likewise the rules of contrariety can be derived via the rules of contradiction and of subalternation. For example:

    (i)   AeB   = assumption
    (ii) AoB   from (i) by rule 16
    (iii) −(AaB) from (ii) by rule 7
Therefore from first to last: AeB ∴ −(AaB)   (= rule 2).

But none of the rules of contradiction can be derived from any combination of the others. Given AaB, AiB can be derived by subalternation, but from AiB it is not possible to reach −(AoB) because AiB and AoB are subcontraries. Likewise, from AaB, −(AeB) can be derived, by contrariety. But from −(AeB) it is not possible to reach −(AoB). This does not suggest that the rules of contradiction in any sense have logical priority over the other rules, but it certainly points to a distinctive logical feature of the relation of contradiction. This distinctive feature is itself connected to a further feature of contradiction which it is appropriate to mention here. Many logicians gave an account of the four relations in the square of opposition in syntactical terms. P and Q are contraries if each implies the negation of the other. They are contradictories if each implies, and is implied by, the negation of the other. They are subcontraries if each is implied by the negation of the other, and P is subalternant to its subalternate Q if P implies Q and not vice versa. Given any proposition there is an indefinite number of other non-equivalent propositions which are contraries of the first proposition. Thus, for example, P&Q has as possible contraries −P, −Q, −P&−Q, (−P&−Q)&R. Likewise a proposition may stand as subalternant in relation to any one of many non-equivalent propositions. For example, P&Q is subalternant in relation to P, Q, PvQ. Likewise a proposition may stand as subcontrary in relation to any one of many non-equivalent propositions. For example, P is subcontrary in relation to −Pv−Q, (−Pv−Q)vR. But there cannot be two non-equivalent propositions each of which is the contradictory of a given proposition. The contradictory of P&Q is either −(P&Q) or any other proposition equivalent to −(P&Q), for example, −Pv−Q. Thus we could form a square of opposition as follows:

$$P\&Q \qquad\qquad -P$$

$$P \qquad\qquad -Pv-Q$$

If we start to construct a square of opposition by placing P&Q as one of the intended subalternants, we have a choice as to which proposition to place as subalternate to P&Q and which to place as contrary to it. But the choice of either fixes what the other will be, because whatever proposition is picked as the contrary of P&Q the negation of that proposition, or an equivalent of that negation, is then the subalternate of P&Q. And whichever proposition is chosen as the subalternate of P&Q, the negation of that subalternate, or a proposition equivalent to that negation, is then the contrary of P&Q. It is the fact that a proposition does not determine its own contrary, subcontrary, subalternant, or subalternate, whereas it determines its own contradictory, that prevents any rules of contradiction being derived from any combination of the rules governing the other sorts of relation. Such determinateness cannot be derived from such indeterminateness.

The Spanish Jewish humanist Juan Luis Vives (1492–1540) wrote an influential treatise, *In Pseudodialecticos*, highly critical of medieval logic in general and of contemporary innovations in particular. Vives, who set as much store by correct Latin as the late John Austin set by correct English, was hostile to the scholastic ideal of a Latin forged as a scientific language. Such a Latin must be in some measure artificial, and for Vives and the other Renaissance humanists schooled in the Roman orators it was even barbaric. For the scholastic logicians, however, the ideal of literary elegance was simply an irrelevance. They were interested in truth rather than beauty, and those ideals could not reasonably be expected to coincide in the medieval logic textbooks. One area of medieval logic Vives singles out for special censure is a late-scholastic development of quantification theory in which artificial quantifiers are introduced. Their artificiality would of course be sufficient to provoke Vives's hostility. But all the same they have features of considerable interest, and it is a particular pity that the 'traditional' logic which developed out of medieval logic should have left them entirely out of account. The artificial quantifiers were represented by single letters from the beginning of the alphabet, and the first four letters, used as quantifiers, were common currency in the decades before the Reformation. Since those quantifiers played a special role in the development of the theory of opposition, this is an appropriate place to consider them. I shall deal in turn with the quantifiers represented by the letters *a*, *b*, *c*, and *d*.

The letter *a* placed immediately before a categorematic term gives merely confused supposition to that term, and its power to give such supposition overrides the power of any other syncategorematic sign to give that term any other sort of supposition. Thus if a term is within the scope of a negation sign, and an *a* is placed immediately before the term, the *a* can be seen as removing the term from the scope of the negation sign. In the plainly false

(i) A man is not an animal

(where the 'A' is the indefinite article) the subject has determinate, and the predicate distributive, supposition. The final descendent of (i) is therefore:

(ii) $(M^1 \neq A^1 \ \& \ M^1 \neq A^2) \ v \ (M^2 \neq A^1 \ \& \ M^2 \neq A^2)$.

In this proposition:

(iii) *a* man is not an animal

'man' has merely confused supposition. Descent is therefore made first under the distributed 'animal', taking us to:

(iv) *a* man is not A^1 & *a* man is not A^2

and then under 'man', taking us to:

(v) $M^1vM^2 \neq A^1$ & $M^1vM^2 \neq A^2$

which is equivalent to

(vi) $(M^1 \neq A^1 \text{ v } M^2 \neq A^1)$ & $(M^1 \neq A^2 \text{ v } M^2 \neq A^2)$.

(vi) states that there is some animal that some man is not, which is true on the assumptions that there are at least two men, and that some animal exists. Given those assumptions, therefore, (iii) is true, though (i) is false. Likewise:

(vii) *a* man is not a man

is true, given that more than one man exists. For the two stages of descent under (vii) are:

(viii) *a* man is not M^1 & *a* man is not M^2
(ix) $M^1vM^2 \neq M^1$ & $M^1vM^2 \neq M^2$

(ix) is equivalent to:

(x) $(M^1 \neq M^1 \text{ v } M^2 \neq M^1)$ & $(M^1 \neq M^2 \text{ v } M^2 \neq M^2)$.

(x) is true, since the second disjunct in the first disjunction and the first disjunct in the second disjunction are both true. And therefore, contrary to first appearances, (vii) is true also.

In some kinds of case *a* has to be introduced at the second stage of descent. For example, in the stock example:

(xi) Of every man an eye is not an eye

(since of every man his right eye is not his left eye) 'man' and the second 'eye' have distributive supposition, and the first 'eye', being indirectly covered by 'every', has merely confused supposition. Descending first under 'man' we reach:

(xii) of M^1 *a* eye is not an eye & Of M^2 *a* eye is not an eye.

In (xii) the *a* is introduced to indicate that the first 'eye' in each of the two conjuncts has merely confused supposition, for the singular M^1 and M^2 cannot by themselves ensure that the 'eye' which they immediately precede has merely confused supposition. Descent is next made under the predicate 'eye' in each conjunct of (xii), and lastly descent is made under the determinable 'eye'. The final descendent of (xii) is:

(xiii) (Of M^1 E^{1}vE$^2\neq$E^1 & Of M^1 E^{1}vE$^2\neq$E^2) &
(Of M^2 E^{1}vE$^2\neq$E^1 & Of M^2 E^{1}vE$^2\neq$E^2)

On this analysis (xi) is true so long as each man has two eyes.

So far in this section we have spoken of the relation of subcontrariety as holding between a particular affirmative and a particular negative proposition. But it might be asked whether a universal proposition can have a subcontrary. The question was duly raised, and one answer given was that:

(xiv) aA is not B

is subcontrary to:

(xv) Every A is B.

As we know, the final descendent of (xv) is:

(xvi) A^1=B^{1}vB^2 & A^2=B^{1}vB^2

which is equivalent to:

(xvii) (A^1=B^1 v A^1=B^2) & (A^2=B^1 v A^2=B^2).

Descent under (xiv) takes us to:

(xviii) aA is not B^1 & aA is not B^2

and thence to:

(xix) A^{1}vA$^2\neq$B^1 & A^{1}vA$^2\neq$B^2

which is equivalent to:

(xx) (A$^1\neq$B^1 v A$^2\neq$B^1) & (A$^1\neq$B^2 v A$^2\neq$B^2).

(xvii) and (xx) are subcontraries. If (xvii) is false, (xx) is true. For if (xvii) is false one of its conjuncts is false. Suppose it to be the first that is false. Its denial is equivalent to:

(xxi) A$^1\neq$B^1 & A$^1\neq$B^2.

The first conjunct of (xxi) implies the first conjunct of (xx), and the second conjunct of (xxi) implies the second conjunct of (xx). Hence

(xxi) implies (xx). Similarly it can be shown that denial of the second conjunct of (xvii) also implies (xx). Therefore the denial of (xvii) implies (xx), and therefore the denial of (xv) implies (xiv). It can be shown by similar means that the denial of (xiv) implies (xv). Additionally, (xvii) and (xx) can be true together, and are on the assumption of

(xxii) $(A^1=B^1 \& A^1\neq B^2) \& (A^2\neq B^1 \& A^2=B^2)$.

Therefore (xiv) and (xv) can also be true together, and therefore (xiv) and (xv) are subcontraries.

We turn now to the second of the artificial quantifiers. b gives determinate supposition to the immediately following categorematic term, and its power to give that supposition cannot be overridden by any other sign. Introducing b into a proposition can change its truth value. William Manderston [*Tripartitum*, g vii] and others gave the example:

(xxiii) Every man is b animal.

Since the predicate has determinate supposition, descent must be made under 'animal' before being made under the distributed subject. Descent takes us to:

(xxiv) Every man is A^1 v Every man is A^2.

Descending now under 'man', we reach:

(xxv) $(M^1=A^1 \& M^2=A^1)$ v $(M^1=A^2 \& M^2=A^2)$

which says that some animal is every man and which therefore is false except on the assumption that there is only one man.

Once a has been introduced into the system there is reason to introduce b, for medieval logicians recognized the importance of being able to specify the contradictory of any given proposition. They wished to know, therefore, what the contradictory of (xiv) was. And since (xiv) was in the canonical form: subject + copula + predicate, they wished its contradictory to be specified in the same form. We have observed that (xiv) is equivalent to (xx). Hence the contradictory of (xx) will also be the contradictory of (xiv). Let us, then, contradict (xx). (xx) negated is equivalent to:

(xxvi) $-(A^1\neq B^1$ v $A^2\neq B^1)$ v $-(A^1\neq B^2$ v $A^2\neq B^2)$

which is equivalent to:

(xxvii) $(A^1=B^1 \ \& \ A^2=B^1) \ v \ (A^1=B^2 \ \& \ A^2=B^2)$.

(xxvii) states that there is some B that every A is. But that is precisely what is stated by:

(xxviii) Every A is bB

as can be verified by observing that (xxviii) and (xxvii) are formally the same as (xxiii) and (xxv) respectively. Therefore the contradictory of (xiv) is (xxviii).

Having fixed the contradictory of (xxviii), let us consider the question of what is contrary to (xxviii). The Dominican philosopher Domingo de Soto gave the answer (*Introductiones Dialectice*, 48^{r-v}):

(xxix) Some A is not B.

Descent under first A and then B in (xxix) takes us to:

(xxx) $(A^1 \neq B^1 \ \& \ A^1 \neq B^2) \ v \ (A^2 \neq B^1 \ \& \ A^2 \neq B^2)$.

The relation between (xxvii) (which spells out (xxviii)) and (xxx) is the relation between:

(xxxi) $(P\&Q)v(R\&S)$

and

(xxxii) $(-P\&-R)v(-Q\&-S)$

respectively. Inspection shows that each of (xxxi) and (xxxii) implies the negation of the other. For example, if (xxxi) is true then one of its disjuncts is true. If the first is true then so are P and Q. If P is true then the first disjunct in (xxxii) is false, and if Q is true then the second disjunct in (xxxii) is false. Hence, given (P&Q), (xxxii) is false. Likewise given R&S (the second disjunct of (xxxi)), (xxxii) is false. By identical means it can be shown that if either disjunct in (xxxii) is true, (xxxi) is false. Also (xxxi) and (xxxii) can be false together, as they are if P and S are true and Q and R are false. Therefore the two schemata are contraries, and therefore so also are (xxviii) and (xxix).

With the artificial quantifiers to hand, further squares of opposition can be constructed. I shall here describe just one, taking as my starting-point:

(xxxiii) No A is bB.

In the absence of b, B would have distributive supposition, but the b

overrides the power of the negation sign to give such supposition. The *b* gives determinate supposition to B, and descent must therefore be made under the B before being made under the distributed A:

(xxxiv) No A is B^1 v No A is B^2

(xxxv) $(A^1 \neq B^1$ & $A^2 \neq B^1)$ v $(A^1 \neq B^2$ & $A^2 \neq B^2)$.

To find the contradictory of (xxxiii) we shall deny (xxxv). Its denial is equivalent to:

(xxxvi) $-(A^1 \neq B^1$ & $A^2 \neq B^1)$ & $-(A^1 \neq B^2$ & $A^2 \neq B^2)$

which is equivalent to:

(xxxvii) $(A^1 = B^1$ v $A^2 = B^1)$ & $(A^1 = B^2$ v $A^2 = B^2)$.

This formula spells out the truth conditions of

(xxxviii) *a*A is every B

for under this last formula descent must be made first under the distributed B and then under the merely confused A, taking us to:

(xxxix) $A^1 v A^2 = B^1$ & $A^1 v A^2 = B^2$

which is equivalent to (xxxvii). Therefore the contradictory of (xxxiii) is (xxxviii).

One formula which implies (xxxvii) in a one-way implication is:

(xl) $(A^1 = B^1$ & $A^2 = B^1)$ & $(A^1 = B^2$ & $A^2 = B^2)$

which gives the truth conditions of

(xli) Every A is every B.

Therefore (xli) is subalternant to (xxxviii).

Let us now look for the contradictory of (xli), and approach the problem by examing (xl). The negation of (xl) is equivalent to:

(xlii) $-(A^1 = B^1$ & $A^2 = B^1)$ v $-(A^1 = B^2$ & $A^2 = B^2)$

which is equivalent to

(xliii) $(A^1 \neq B^1$ v $A^2 \neq B^1)$ v $(A^1 \neq B^2$ v $A^2 \neq B^2)$.

This gives the truth condition of

(xliv) Some A is not *b*B

for in (xliv) A and B each have determinate supposition. Let us descend first under B:

(xlv) Some A is not B^1 v Some A is not B^2.

And descent under A takes us to (xliii). Hence (xli) and (xliv) are contradictories.

Additionally (xli) and (xxxiii) are contraries as can be seen by inspection of (xl) and (xxxv) which give their respective truth conditions. (xxxviii) and (xliv) are subcontraries as inspection of (xxxvii) and (xliii) reveals. And finally, (xxxiii) is subalternant to (xliv). These relations are represented in the following square of opposition:

(1) Every A is every B   (3) No A is *b*B

(2) *a*A is every B   (4) Some A is not *b*B

Other such squares can be constructed. But we shall turn now instead to an examination of more complex artificial quantifiers, which in their turn led to the construction of squares of opposition appreciably more complex than the one just described.

The more complex artificial quantifiers were particularly prominent in discussions concerning the possessive construction. Late-scholastic logicians had a lively interest in possessives. For example, Lokert specified the rules which permit such inferences as: 'Some man's donkey is running and every donkey is a quadruped. Therefore some man's quadruped is running', and 'Every donkey is a quadruped and some runner is a man's donkey. Therefore some runner is a man's quadruped' (see *Sill.* 4vb). Possessives, however, give rise to logical problems. For example, the following two arguments seem to have the same form: 'Brunellus is yours and Brunellus is a donkey. Therefore Brunellus is your donkey' and 'Brunellus is yours and Brunellus is a father. Therefore Brunellus is your father.' Yet the first appears to be valid and the latter not. Or is the first not in fact valid? What, then, is wrong with it? Problems concerning possessives are not related solely to the employment of possessive pronouns. What, for example, should be said about this inference: 'Any mother-in-law is a parent. Jane is Mary's mother-in-law. Therefore Jane is Mary's parent'? I give these examples to illustrate the point that the logic of possessives is only very imperfectly understood. Medieval logicians seem not to have noticed some problems which now trouble us, though they certainly faced up to others. For the remainder of this section I shall deal with aspects of that corner of their theory of possessives which involves complex artificial quantifiers.

c and *d* are quantifiers conferring mixed supposition. They can occur only in categorical propositions containing at least three categorematic terms. We are concerned here, therefore, with propositions displaying such forms as:

(xlvi) Every A of some B is C
(xlvii) Of some A every B is C
(xlviii) Every A is some B's C
(xlix) Some A is every B of every C.

The letter *c* immediately preceding the third categorematic term indicates that that term should be taken to have merely confused supposition in relation to the first term and to have determinate supposition in relation to the second. This has an immediate effect on the order in which descent is to be made under the three terms. In (xlvii) the order of descent is this: first under A, then under B, and finally under C, since those terms have respectively determinate, distributive, and merely confused supposition. In:

(l) Of some A every B is *c*C

C has merely confused supposition in relation to A which is determinate, and it has determinate supposition in relation to B which is distributed. The order of descent is therefore as follows: first under A which has determinate supposition, then under C which is determinate in relation to B, and finally under B which is distributed. The three stages of descent under (l) are therefore these:

(li) Of A¹ every B is *b*C v Of A² every B is *b*C

(Here *b* occurs rather than *c*, to indicate that C has determinate supposition in relation to B.)

(lii) (Of A¹ every B is C¹ v Of A¹ every B is C²) v
(Of A² every B is C¹ v Of A² every B is C²)

(liii) [(Of A¹ B¹=C¹ & Of A¹ B²=C¹) v
(Of A¹ B¹=C² & Of A¹ B²=C²)] v
[(Of A² B¹=C¹ & Of A² B²=C¹) v
(Of A² B¹=C² & Of A² B²=C²)].

We turn lastly to the quantifier *d*. When it immediately precedes the third categorematic term in a categorical proposition it indicates that that term has determinate supposition in relation to the first term and has merely confused supposition in relation to the second. Thus the *d* in:

(liv) Every A of every B is *d*C

indicates that C has determinate supposition in relation to A (and therefore descent should be made under C before being made under A), and has merely confused supposition in relation to B (and therefore descent should be made under B before being made under C). Descent, therefore, is to be made under B, C, and A, in that order. The three stages of descent are as follows:

(lv) Every A of B¹ is *b*C & Every A of B² is *b*C

(Here *b* occurs at the first stage of descent to indicate that C has determinate supposition in relation to A.)

(lvi) (Every A of B¹ is C¹ v Every A of B¹ is C²) &
       (Every A of B² is C¹ v Every A of B² is C²)
(lvii) [(A¹ of B¹=C¹ & A² of B¹=C¹) v
       (A¹ of B¹=C² & A² of B¹=C²)] &
       [(A¹ of B²=C¹ & A² of B²=C¹) v
       (A¹ of B²=C² & A² of B²=C²)].

In the light of this explanation of *d* let us now search for contraries as the late-scholastic logicians did, and in particular let us examine:

(lviii) Of every A every B is not C.

A, B, and C all have distributive supposition. Descent should be made under A before being made under B in accordance with the rule that where a complex phrase consists of a determinant and a determinable which each have the same kind of supposition, the determinant has priority over the determinable in the order of descent. We shall descend first under A, then under B, and finally under C:

(lix)   Of A¹ every B is not C & Of A² every B is not C
(lx)   (Of A¹ B¹ is not C & Of A¹ B² is not C) &
        (Of A² B¹ is not C & Of A² B² is not C)
(lxi) [(Of A¹ B¹≠C¹ & Of A¹ B¹≠C²) &
        (Of A¹ B²≠C¹ & Of A¹ B²≠C²)] &

$$[(\text{Of } A^2 \ B^1 \neq C^1 \ \& \ \text{Of } A^2 \ B^1 \neq C^2) \ \&$$
$$(\text{Of } A^2 \ B^2 \neq C^1 \ \& \ \text{Of } A^2 \ B^2 \neq C^2) \ ].$$

A contrary of (lviii) is the following:

(lxii) Of every A every B is cC.

The c indicates that C has merely confused supposition in relation to A and determinate supposition in relation to B. The order of descent is therefore as follows: first under the distributed A, then under the determinate C, and finally under the distributed B. The following are the stages of descent under (lxii):

(lxiii) Of A^1 every B is bC & Of A^2 every B is bC

(The b indicates that C is determinate in relation to B.)

(lxiv) (Of A^1 every B is C^1 v Of A^1 every B is C^2) &
   (Of A^2 every B is C^1 v Of A^2 every B is C^2)

(lxv) $[(\text{Of } A^1 \ B^1 = C^1 \ \& \ \text{Of } A^1 \ B^2 = C^1) \ v$
   $(\text{Of } A^1 \ B^1 = C^2 \ \& \ \text{Of } A^1 \ B^2 = C^2) \ ] \ \&$
   $[(\text{Of } A^2 \ B^1 = C^1 \ \& \ \text{Of } A^2 \ B^2 = C^1) \ v$
   $(\text{Of } A^2 \ B^1 = C^2 \ \& \ \text{Of } A^2 \ B^2 = C^2) \ ].$

Each of (lxi) and (lxv) implies the negation of the other. And additionally both can be false together, as for example when this holds:

(lxvi) (Of A^1 $B^1 = C^1$ & Of A^1 $B^2 \neq C^1$) and Of A^1 $B^1 \neq C^2$.

Therefore (lxii) is a contrary of (lviii). By similar means it can be shown that

(lxvii) Of aA every B is not C

and

(lxviii) Of every A every B is dC

are contraries.

These points complete my exposition of the four relations of opposition. I should like to turn now to a consideration of the various relations of equipollence. As will quickly become obvious, the notions of opposition and equipollence are very closely related.

II. *Equipollence*

Given that of two propositions one is contradictory, contrary, subaltern, or subcontrary to the other, then the question can be raised: By what (if any) placing of negation signs in the first proposition is it transformed into a proposition equivalent to the second? The rules of equipollence provide an answer to this question. There are four sets of rules of equipollence, corresponding to the four kinds of relation exhibited in the square of opposition

Peter of Spain writes: 'If to some [universal or particular] sign a negation is prefixed then [the proposition] is equipollent to its contradictory' (*Tractatus*, p. 10). That is, if two propositions are contradictories then by placing a negation in front of the sign of quantity in one of the propositions those propositions become equipollent. Therefore 'Every A is B', which is the contradictory of 'Some A is not B', is equipollent to 'Not some A is not B.' 'Some A is B', which is the contradictory of 'Every A is not B' (= 'No A is B'), is equipollent to 'Not every A is not B.' Using ↔ to symbolize 'is equivalent to', the full list of rules of equipollence, as applied to contradictories, is as follows:

(17) AaB ↔ −(AoB)
(18) Aeb ↔ −(AiB)
(19) AiB ↔ −(AeB)
(20) AoB ↔ −(AaB).

The negation sign here is straightforwardly a sign negating the whole proposition, and there is no impropriety in placing it at the start of the proposition. But where a negation sign renders contraries equipollent, the matter is not quite so straightforward. The rule is: 'If a negation sign is placed after some universal sign then [the proposition] is equipollent to its contrary' (Peter of Spain, *Tractatus*, p. 10). Thus, 'Every A is B', which is contrary to 'No A is B', is equipollent to 'No A is not B.' Here we are to understand 'not' as including in its scope 'is B'. The view that medieval logicians took of a negation sign so placed in a proposition was that by operating on the copula it reversed the quality of the proposition, but that since it did not operate on the initial quantifier it did not affect the quantity. Thus, inserting 'not' after the subject in 'No A is B' transforms the original proposition into one which retains the original quantity (universal) but reverses the quality (which had been negative). Hence 'No A is not B' is equipollent to the universal affirmative 'Every A is B.'

The negation placed in the proposition after the subject is a sign of propositional negation, since its insertion in an affirmative proposition transforms it into a negative proposition, and its insertion in a singly negative proposition transforms it into a proposition equivalent to one which is affirmative. Certainly there is no question that the negation is of the infinitizing variety. For this reason it is permissible to use the same sign to symbolize 'not' after the subject as is used to symbolize a negation at the beginning of a proposition whose next term is a quantifier. The rules of equipollence as applied to contrary propositions can therefore be expressed as follows:

(21) AaB ↔ Ae−B
(22) AeB ↔ Aa−B.

Both kinds of negation just discussed are invoked in specifying the rules of equipollence as applied to subaltern propositions: 'If a negation sign is placed both before and after the universal or particular sign, [the proposition] is equipollent to its subaltern' (Peter of Spain, *Tractatus*, p. 10). Thus, 'Every A is B', which is subalternant to 'Some A is B', is equipollent to 'Not some A is not B'. 'Not some A is B' is equivalent to 'No A is B.' To insert a predicate negation in 'No A is B' transforms that proposition, as we have seen, into one equivalent to a universal affirmative. Likewise 'Some A is not B', which is subalternate to 'Every A is not B', is equipollent to 'Not every A is not not B', that is, 'Not every A is B', that is, 'Some A is not B.' The rules of equipollence, as applied to subalterns, can be expressed as:

(23) Aab ↔ −(Ai−B)
(24) AeB ↔ −(Ao−B)
(25) AiB ↔ −(Aa−B)
(26) AoB ↔ −(Ae−B).

During the fourteenth century, discussion of rules of equipollence did not include an account of how subcontraries are to be transformed into equipollent propositions. It is possible that it was taken for granted that the rules given for transforming contraries would be seen to apply to the rules for transforming subcontraries. It is also possible, though less likely, that it was not realized that subcontraries could be transformed into equipollents. Though if it was thought that they could not be so transformed, this would surely have prompted the question of why this was so. But in any case, on the basis of the foregoing discussion it is easy to construct the rules of equipollence as applied to subcontraries.

(27) AiB ↔ Ao−B
(28) AoB ↔ Ai−B.

As can be seen, the rules concerning the transformation of contraries into equipollents apply in exactly the same way to subcontraries.

It is difficult to say rule 28 aloud in such a way as to present the logical point being made. AoB and Ai−B are both read most naturally as 'Some A is not B'. The same problem occurs in Latin, and this fact about the Latin rendering may have contributed to the lack of discussion on the relation between equipollence and subcontrariety.

Before leaving the topic of equipollence, I should like to deal with the following objection: Chapter 8, Section I, contains a discussion concerning existential import. It was stated there that an affirmative categorical proposition, whether universal or particular, implies the existence of a significate of the subject and of the predicate, but a negative categorical does not. Indeed a negative categorical is true if either the subject or the predicate does not have an existing significate. How, then, can two propositions be equipollent if one is affirmative and the other negative? For example, how can 27 be justified given that if no A exists, then AiB, being affirmative, is false, and Ao−B, being negative, is true? The answer is to be derived from Burley's discussion (see Chapter 7, Section I) concerning categorical propositions with two negation signs of which one is within the scope of the other. Such negative propositions are equivalent, he argues, to affirmative propositions. If a categorical proposition is negative in virtue of containing a single negation sign, then it is true if either its subject or its predicate does not signify any existing thing. If a categorical proposition is negative in virtue of containing two negation signs of which one is within the scope of the other, then its equivalence to an affirmative proposition ensures that if either extreme does not signify any existing thing the proposition is false. Hence Ao−B is false if there exists no A or no B, just as AiB (which is equipollent to Ao−B) is false if either of those conditions is satisfied.

III. *Conversion*

A conversion is a valid inference consisting of two propositions, both categorical, one the premiss, called the 'convertend', and the other the conclusion, called the 'converse'. The subject and the predicate in the convertend recur as the predicate and the subject respectively in the converse. The theory of conversion sets out to answer two main questions: given a true categorical proposition, does replacement of the subject by the predicate and the predicate by the subject result, for logical reasons, in another true proposition, and if not then what other changes need to be made to the first proposition to ensure, on logical grounds, the preservation of truth? Three kinds of conversion were discussed, simple, accidental, and contrapositive, though, as we shall see, there are reasons, recognized by some medieval logicians, for denying that contrapositive conversion is, strictly speaking, a variety of conversion. But contrapositive conversion was always classed as a kind of conversion, even if only a rather degenerate kind, and for that reason I shall examine it after dealing with the simple and the accidental varieties.

Simple conversion first. This is a conversion in which the converse has the same quantity and quality as the convertend. Two kinds of proposition were each said to be simply convertible, the particular affirmative and the universal negative. The following are, therefore, rules of valid inference:

(29) AiB ∴ BiA
(30) AeB ∴ BeA.

In the light of the doctrine of supposition it is possible to pinpoint the underlying logical features of those kinds of proposition that ensure their simple convertibility. Let us assume, as usual, that A^1 and A^2 are the only things that are A, and B^1 and B^2 the only things that are B. Descent to singulars under first the subject and then the predicate in the premiss of rule 29 takes us to:

(i) $(A^1=B^1 \text{ v } A^1=B^2) \text{ v } (A^2=B^1 \text{ v } A^2=B^2)$.

Descending to singulars first under the predicate and then under the subject of the conclusion of rule 29 takes us to:

(ii) $(B^1=A^1 \text{ v } B^2=A^1) \text{ v } (B^1=A^2 \text{ v } B^2=A^2)$.

To each disjunct in the one disjunction there corresponds one disjunct in the other differing only in the order of the extremes. But the relation of identity is commutative, that is, for any x and any y, if x = y then y = x, a point Ockham puts (*Summa Logicae*, II 21) by saying that a singular affirmative proposition can be converted into a singular affirmative proposition. The example he gives is 'Socrates is Plato. Therefore Plato is Socrates.' Hence (i) and (ii) are deducible from each other. It is clear that however large the domain, the descendents of AiB and BiA will be mutually deducible. And it is this logical feature of the identity relation that ultimately underlies the simple convertibility of particular affirmatives.

Precisely the same point can be made about the simple convertibility of universal negatives. Assuming the same domain as before, descent first under the subject and then under the predicate of the premiss in rule 30 takes us to:

(iii) $(A^1 \neq B^1 \ \& \ A^1 \neq B^2) \ \& \ (A^2 \neq B^1 \ \& \ A^2 \neq B^2)$.

Descent first under the predicate and then under the subject in the conclusion in rule 30 takes us to:

(iv) $(B^1 \neq A^1 \ \& \ B^2 \neq A^1) \ \& \ (B^1 \neq A^2 \ \& \ B^2 \neq A^2)$.

Once again there is a one-to-one correspondence of the descendants of the two categorical propositions. And since non-identity is commutative (for any x and y, if $x \neq y$ then $y \neq x$), it follows that (iii) and (iv) follow from each other. Whatever the size of the domain the descendants of AeB and BeA will be mutually deducible. AeB is therefore simply convertible, and it is the commutativity of the non-identity relation that underlies this feature of universal negatives.

Each of rules 29 and 30 can be derived from the other along with certain other rules already accepted. Let us assume rule 29. If an inference is valid the negation of its premiss follows from the negation of its conclusion. Therefore the following must also be valid:

(29a) $-(BiA) \ \therefore \ -(AiB)$.

But by rules 5 and 9 (Ch. 8), $-(BiA)$ and $-(AiB)$ are equivalent respectively to BeA and AeB. By substitution of equivalents for equivalents in rule 29a we reach:

(29b) BeA $\therefore$ AeB.

Since 29b is formally valid, its validity is preserved if categorematic terms are replaced systematically. Replace B by A, and A by B. Then this is sound:

(29c) AeB $\therefore$ BeA   = rule 30   Q.E.D.

Rule 29 can be derived from rule 30 in the same way.

The two kinds of conversion just described are both simple and mutual; simple in that convertend and converse have the same quality and quantity, mutual in that convertend and converse follow from each other. Ockham (*Summa Logicae*, II 21) mentions a wider sense of 'simple conversion', namely 'mutual conversion'. For a conversion can be mutual without being simple in the narrow sense. Ockham has in mind a singular proposition and a particular proposition with which it is convertible. 'Socrates is a man' converts mutually with 'Some man is Socrates.' But the conversion is not 'simple' in the original sense, since convertend and converse do not have the same quantity. In Ockham's view, at any rate, singularity is not the same quantity as particularity. In so far as he did not think of singularity as a third kind of quantity alongside the other two he thought of it as identifiable with universality rather than with particularity—if Socrates is a man then *everything* which is Socrates is a man.

We turn next to accidental conversion. Here the converse has the same quality as the convertend but not the same quantity. Both a universal affirmative and a universal negative proposition can be converted in this way. Thus the following are rules of valid inference:

(31) AaB ∴ BiA
(32) AeB ∴ BoA.

The soundness of these two rules can be displayed by descending to singulars under the premiss and conclusion of each of them, and considering the logical relations between the descendants. But rules 31 and 32 can in any case be derived from rules already established. The derivations are as follows:

  (i) AaB = assumption
 (ii) AiB from (i) by rule 15 (Ch. 8)
(iii) BiA from (ii) by rule 29 (Ch. 8).
Therefore from first to last: AaB ∴ BiA   = rule 31.

 (iv) AeB = assumption
 (v) BeA from (iv) by rule 30 (Ch. 8)
(vi) BoA from (v) by rule 16 (Ch. 8).
Therefore from first to last: AeB ∴ BoA   = rule 32.

Unlike simple conversion, accidental conversion is not mutual. Consideration of the foregoing two proofs reveals that the reason for this is that the inference from subalternant to subalternate (steps (ii) and (vi) above) is one-way only.

We have not so far identified any categorical proposition with which 'Every A is B' is mutually convertible, but one such proposition is readily to hand if use is made of one of the artificial quantifiers introduced in Chapter 8, Section I. In:

(i) Every A is B

the predicate has, as we know, merely confused supposition. In Section I we introduced the quantifier a whose role is to confer merely confused supposition on the immediately following categorematic term. Reversing (i) by transforming it into:

(ii) aB is every A

results in a proposition whose subject has the same kind of supposition as the predicate of (i), and whose predicate has the same kind of supposition as the subject of (i). Since in (ii) A is distributed, descent must be made under that term before being made under the merely confused B. The final descendant is therefore:

(iii) $B^1vB^2=A^1$ & $B^1vB^2=A^2$

which is equivalent to:

(iv) $(B^1=A^1vB^2=A^1)$ & $(B^1=A^2vB^2=A^2)$.

Since identity is a commutative relation (iv) is equivalent to:

(v) $(A^1=B^1vA^1=B^2)$ & $(A^2=B^1vA^2=B^2)$.

But (v) also gives the truth conditions of (i), and hence (i) and (ii) are mutually convertible. But the conversion, though mutual, is not strictly speaking simple, since convertend and converse, though the same in quality, are different in quantity. Medieval logicians did not indeed provide a word to describe the quantity of (ii). It is certainly not universal since the subject is undistributed. Neither is it particular or indefinite since the subject is not determinate. Perhaps we should say that (ii) is merely confused. But whatever name we use, it is clear that on the standard account of 'simple conversion' the conversion with which we are here dealing is not simple. If however we revised the original conception of simple conversion and said instead that a conversion is simple if the supposition of the subject and predicate in the convertend is the same as the supposition of the predicate and subject respectively in the converse (as is the case with AiB and AeB, each of which is simply convertible), then (i) and (ii) are, after all, simply as well as mutually convertible.

It should be added that even without the use of the artificial quantifier *a*, we can construct a converse of 'Every A is B' which is mutually convertible with the convertend. The converse in question is 'Only B is A.' But in this case, also, the conversion is not simple if a simple conversion is one in which the convertend and the converse have the same quantity. For it was held (see, for example, Paul of Venice, *Logica*, p. 7) that exclusive propositions (that is, roughly, those of the form 'Only A is B', 'Only A is not B', and their negations) have no quantity.

Finally we must consider contrapositive conversion. Such conversion was investigated in the first place in an attempt to solve the problem of how particular negative propositions are to be converted. AoB is not convertible into BeA, as is obvious. Neither is it convertible into BoA, for 'Some logic book is not a book' is not a valid converse of 'Some book is not a logic book.' The proposition is therefore neither simply nor accidentally convertible. The problem was solved, at least provisionally, by the invention of contrapositive conversion. Peter of Spain writes:

Contrapositive conversion is making the predicate out of the subject and the subject out of the predicate, while keeping the quality and quantity, but changing finite terms into infinite terms. Universal affirmatives and particular negatives are converted in this way. (*Tractatus*, p. 8)

Where $-(T)$ signifies the negation of the term T, the two rules indicated by Peter of Spain can be expressed as:

(33) AaB ∴ $-(B)a-(A)$
(34) AoB ∴ $-(B)o-(A)$.

For example, given that some animal is not a man it does not follow that some man is not an animal, but it does follow that some non-man is not a non-animal. If some animal, say the donkey Brunellus, is not a man then some non-man, namely Brunellus, is not a non-animal. And if every man is an animal then every non-animal is a non-man.

Peter of Spain expressed no qualms about this type of conversion, but subsequent generations of logicians were less happy about the validity of rules 33 and 34.

When turning from a consideration of general rules of inference to those involving inference of one categorical proposition from another, Albert of Saxony lays down, as his first rule, that no contrapositive conversion is a formal inference (*Perutilis Logica*, 25[vb]). The positioning of this rule suggests a context of lively debate on contrapositives. In justification of his rule, Albert furnishes counter-examples to rules 33 and 34 above. First, as regards 33, let us, at Albert's suggestion, consider:

(i) Every man is an entity.

According to 33 this should imply:

(ii) Every non-entity is a non-man.

But unlike (i), (ii) is false. Since there are no non-entities there is no non-entity which is a non-man. (ii) is false, therefore, in accordance with the principle that every affirmative proposition with a subject which does not supposit for anything is false.

Secondly, as regards rule 34, Albert gives the example:

(iii) Some chimera is not a man.

According to rule 34 this should imply:

(iv) Some non-man is not a non-chimera.

But (iii) is true and (iv) false. That (iii) is true follows from the principle that every negative proposition with a subject which does not supposit for anything is true. Since no chimera exists there is no chimera to be a man, and therefore, by subalternation, some chimera is not a man. (iv) is false because its contradictory is true. Its contradictory is:

(v) Every non-man is a non-chimera.

Since everything is a non-chimera, every non-man is one.

Conversions are not merely valid inferences, they are formally valid and therefore their validity is invariant through systematic replacement of categorematic terms in the convertend and the converse. It follows from this that: 'Every man is an animal. Therefore every non-animal is a non-man', even if valid, is not formally so, and neither is: 'Some animal is not a man. Therefore some non-man is not a non-animal.' But if we wish to insist that, formally or not, these two last sample arguments are valid, it follows that they are enthymemes. What, then, are the missing premisses?

Attempts to convert (i) and (iii) contrapositively fail for opposite reasons. In the case of (i) the predicate is a transcendental term, that is, a term which is truly predicable of anything whatever that exists, and infinitizing it results in a term which, placed as a subject in an affirmative proposition, ensures the falsity of the proposition, whereas in the case of (iii) the subject stands for nothing, and therefore infinitizing it results in a transcendental term. But any negative proposition, in which a transcendental term is predicated of a term signifying something that exists, must be false. Contrapositive conversion fails, therefore, because no restriction is placed on the categorematic terms in the convertend. Since in the case of (i) the problem arises because the predicate when infinitized stands for nothing, along with the universal affirmative proposition an additional premiss must be placed in the inference, affirming that there exists something of which that infinitized predicate is truly predicable. Thus we can argue validly: 'Every man is an animal. There is a non-animal. Therefore every non-animal is a non-man.' This is formally valid. Hence this also is valid: 'Every man is an entity. There is a non-entity. Therefore every non-entity is a non-man.' It is granted that the conclusion is false, but so also is the second premiss. And consequently nothing false is being inferred from something true.

Since in the case of (iii) the problem arises because the subject stands for nothing, along with the particular negative proposition an additional premiss must be placed affirming that there exists something for which the subject of the first premiss stands. Thus we can argue validly: 'Some animal is not a man. There is an animal. Therefore some non-man is not a non-animal.' This is formally valid. Hence this also is valid: 'Some chimera is not a man. There exists a chimera. Therefore some non-man is not a non-chimera.' It is granted that the conclusion is false, but so also is the second premiss. And consequently something false is not being inferred from something true.

Albert of Saxony was aware of these moves. He writes: 'Contrapositive conversion is a formal inference on the hypothesis or assumption that every one of its terms stands for something' (*Perutilis Logica*, 26[ra]). But it has to be added that what he now says is a formal inference is not a contrapositive conversion in the original sense of the phrase. For conversion has, by definition, a single premiss, the convertend, and contrapositive conversion, if presented as a real conversion, that is, with only the convertend as premiss, is not formally valid but is instead an enthymeme whose suppressed premiss asserts the existence of something for which an extreme of the convertend stands.

One might try to get round this point by restricting the categorematic terms available to logicians so that they do not have access either to transcendental terms or to terms which do not stand for anything.

Given such restrictions, any inference from a universal affirmative or particular negative to its contrapositive converse would go through smoothly. But two points should be made about this proposal. First, it runs counter to the entire spirit of medieval logic, for logicians took as their object language the whole of natural language, not just the parts or features of it that did not cause problems for logicians—they had, of course, a particular interest in the parts or features which *did* cause them problems. Secondly, the proposal would require very drastic reduction indeed in the resources available to logicians. For as we have seen, they investigated the logic of compound terms, terms such as those constructed by placing a disjunction or conjunction sign between categorematic terms. And given this use of disjunction and conjunction signs, and the use of an infinitizing negation sign, it was easy for them to construct, as they did, transcendental terms and terms which cannot stand for anything, for example, 'man or non-man' and 'man and non-man', the former of which is predicable of everything and the latter of nothing.

I should like to make a further point about the conversion of particular negatives. In:

(i) Some A is not B

A has determinate supposition and B is distributed. It is possible to reverse (i) in such a way that B occurs as a distributed subject and A as a determinate predicate, while the transformed proposition is, like (i), negative:

(ii) Every B is not *b* A.

In (ii) descent should be made first under A and then under B. The two stages of descent under (ii) are:

(iii) Every B is not A^1 v Every B is not A^2
(iv) $(B^1 \neq A^1 \& B^2 \neq A^1)$ v $(B^1 \neq A^2 \& B^2 \neq A^2)$.

Since the non-identity relation is commutative, (iv) is equivalent to:

(v) $(A^1 \neq B^1 \& A^1 \neq B^2)$ v $(A^2 \neq B^1 \& A^2 \neq B^2)$.

(v) also gives the truth conditions of (i). Hence (i) and (ii) are mutually convertible. But if we retain the conception of simple conversion as a conversion whose convertend and converse have the same quantity and quality, then the conversion with which we are here dealing is not simple, since (i) is a particular proposition and (ii) is universal. If however we adopt a suggestion made earlier in this section, and say instead that a conversion is simple if the supposition of the subject and predicate in the convertend is the same as the supposition of the predicate and subject respectively in the converse, then (i) and (ii) are simply convertible with each other. And on that basis the relation between them is the same as the relation between 'Every A is B' and '*a*B is every A.'

All the rules of conversion so far given relate to propositions containing no ampliative terms, and it cannot be assumed that all, or even any, of those rules apply to propositions whose copulas are non-present-tensed or whose predicates have ampliative power. Examples should make plain that propositions with ampliative terms provide exceptions to our rules. Particular affirmative propositions convert simply. Let us consider, then, this proposition:

(i) A man is dead.

'Dead', used as a predicate in an affirmative proposition with a copula in the present tense, ampliates the subject to supposit for what is or was. The subject in (i) does not supposit for what is a man, since, according to a standard doctrine inherited from Aristotle, dead men are not men. So (i) implies:

(ii) What is or was a man is dead.

It follows that (i) cannot be converted simply into:

(iii) A dead thing is a man

for (i) is true and (iii) false.

Again, universal negatives were said to be simply convertible. Let us, then, consider this example:

(iv) No white thing was a man.

It might seem that a converse of (iv) is:

(v) No man was white.

In (iv) the subject is ampliated to stand for what is or was white. Let us suppose that it stands for what *is* white. Let us suppose in addition (a) that only two white things W^1 and W^2 have ever existed of which at past time t^1 both existed, (b) that now W^1 is the only existing white thing, (c) that only one man M ever existed, and he exists now, (d) that M was W^2, and (e) that M was not and is not W^1. On this hypothesis

(iv) is true since each of the singular propositions 'This which is white was not a man' is true, for nothing we can now point to while saying truly 'This is white' was a man. But (v) is false, for it is laid down in the hypothesis that M was W^2.

It follows that the rules for conversion require to be modified to deal with propositions containing ampliative terms. Let us stay with past-tensed propositions in which the subject is a common term. The subject can supposit for what is or for what was. The rules for conversion include the following: if the subject supposits for what is then the proposition should not be converted into a past-tensed proposition but into a present-tensed proposition in which the subject is taken with the verb 'was' and the pronoun 'which' (see Ockham, *Summa Logicae*, II 22). Therefore (iv) converts into:

(vi) Nothing which was a man is white.

This rule does not apply to (i) since there the subject cannot be taken to supposit for what is.

If, on the other hand, the subject is taken to supposit for what was, then the proposition is converted simply into a past-tensed proposition. Let us suppose, for example, that in (iv) 'white' is taken to supposit for what was white, then (iv) converts into:

(vii) No man was white.

Since in (i) the subject must be taken to supposit for what was a man, (i) converts into:

(viii) A dead thing was a man.

So far we have considered ampliated propositions whose subject is a common term. A different, and rather simpler, account of conversion can be given for such propositions whose subject is a proper name. The crucial difference between, say, 'A white thing was a man' and 'Socrates was a man' is that what we now point to and call 'Socrates' always was Socrates so long as he existed. But what we now point to and call 'a white thing' might have existed in the past without then being white. Hence a past-tensed singular proposition, say:

(ix) Socrates was not white

is converted into a proposition in which the subject is taken for what was:

(x) Nothing which was white was Socrates.

The subject must be taken for what was, for otherwise fallacies occur. If (x) were replaced as the converse of (ix) by:

(xi) Nothing which is white was Socrates

then the conversion is invalid. For if Socrates had never been white but is now white for the first time, then (ix) is true and (xi) false.

The points just made about the convertibility of past-tensed propositions apply, with obvious adaptations, to future-tensed propositions also. No important new principle arises with the necessary adaptations.

For the present we shall leave the topic of conversion and shall turn next to the large subject of syllogistic inference. But rules stated in this chapter will remain much to the fore since, as we shall see, the proof procedures for syllogisms include rules of subalternation and conversion, as well as other rules we have discussed.

9
Syllogistic Tense Logic

I. *Elementary syllogistic*

The term 'syllogism' was used in a wide sense to signify any piece of reasoning, theoretical or practical. Within the area of theoretical reasoning a distinction was drawn between categorical and molecular syllogisms. A molecular syllogism is distinguished by the presence of at least one molecular proposition occurring as a premiss. In a categorical syllogism each proposition, whether premiss or conclusion, is categorical. In the *Prior Analytics* Aristotle made a systematic study of categorical syllogisms, focusing there on syllogisms containing just two premisses, the first the 'major' premiss and the second the 'minor', where the categorical conclusion relates an extreme of one premiss to an extreme of the other. The two extremes could be thus related in the conclusion because of the role played by a term which occurs twice in the premisses, once in each premiss. This term, the 'middle term', mediates between the two other extremes in the premisses.

The theory of the syllogism expounded by Aristotle was taken up by medieval logicians and extended in a variety of directions. The largest part of what is now commonly thought of as 'traditional' logic is a small fragment of medieval syllogistic. I do not wish to say a great deal about 'traditional' logic for there are many expositions available, such as that by J. M. Keynes in his *Formal Logic*. My chief concern here with medieval syllogistic is with areas of that theory which did not find their way into the subsequent 'traditional' logic. But I would prefer first to set out some of the elementary parts of the medieval account; to set it out, however, in the light of what the medieval logicians, rather than their successors, said. The brief description of certain of the elementary parts should provide a basis, sufficient for immediate purposes, on which to construct an account of the role played in valid syllogisms by propositions with ampliative terms. In particular I shall attend to the question of whether there can be valid syllogisms containing non-present-tensed premisses.

First, then, to cover well-trodden ground. Since we are dealing with inferences composed of two categorical premisses and a categorical conclusion, and the premisses share an extreme which is absent from the conclusion, we have to deal with four varieties of pairs of premisses, viz. those in which the middle term is (i) subject in the major premiss and predicate in the minor, (ii) predicate in both premisses, (iii) subject in both premisses, and (iv) predicate in the major premiss and subject in the minor. A categorical syllogism is said to be of the first, second, third, or fourth figure according as its premisses answer to the description in (i), (ii), (iii), or (iv) respectively.

Of valid syllogistic forms four had a special status, for on their basis the validity of every valid syllogism, of whatever form, was to be established. The four valid forms were themselves established on the basis of two 'regulative principles' of syllogistic, namely, the rules *dici de omni* and *dici de nullo*. There is a great deal of logic to be coaxed out of these principles. The first asserts that what is said of a distributed subject is said of everything of which that subject is truly predicated. The second asserts that what is denied of a distributed subject is denied of everything of which that subject is truly predicated.

In AaB the subject is distributed. Hence, by *dici de omni*, if A is truly predicated of every C then what is said of A, namely B, is truly predicated of every C, and if A is truly predicated of some C then what is said of A, namely B, is truly predicated of some C. In AeB the subject is distributed. Hence, by *dici de nullo*, if A is truly predicated of every C then what is denied of A, namely B, is truly predicated of no C, and if A is truly predicated of some C then what is denied of A, namely B, is truly denied of some C. The four syllogistic forms thus generated are as follows (I add their medieval names in brackets):

(i)   AaB & CaA ∴ CaB   (= *Barbara*)
(ii) AaB & CiA ∴ CiB   (= *Darii*)
(iii) AeB & CaA ∴ CeB   (= *Celarent*)
(iv) AeB & CiA ∴ CoB   (= *Ferio*).

In addition to these four syllogistic forms, rules of immediate inference, in particular, those of conversion, equipollence, and subalternation, were employed in proving the validity of syllogisms, as also were four rules (63–6 in Chapter 7) which were invoked to prove syllogisms *per impossibile*, that is, to prove syllogisms by assuming one of the premisses and the negation of the conclusion, and proving the negation of the other premiss. I shall set out some proofs in illustration of the medieval method.

To prove: AeB & CaB ∴ CoA   (= *Cesaro*)

  (i)   AeB & CaB = assumption
  (ii) AeB   from (i) by rule 49 (Ch. 7)
  (iii) CaB   from (i) by rule 50 (Ch. 7)
  (iv) BeA   from (ii) by simple conversion
  (v)   BeA & CaB from (iv), (iii), from two propositions to their conjunction
  (vi) CeA   from (v) by *Celarent*
  (vii) CoA   from (vi) by subalternation
Therefore from first to last: AeB & CaB ∴ CoA   Q.E.D.

To prove: AaB & AaC ∴ CiB   (= *Darapti*)

  (i)   AaB & AaC = assumption
  (ii) AaB   from (i) by rule 49 (Ch. 7)
  (iii) AaC   from (i) by rule 50 (Ch. 7)
  (iv) CiA   from (iii) by accidental conversion
  (v)   AaB & CiA from (ii), (iv), from two propositions to their conjunction
  (vi) CiB   from (v) by *Darii*
Therefore from first to last: AaB & AaC ∴ CiB   Q.E.D.

To prove: AeB & BaC ∴ CoA   (= *Fesapo*)

  (i)   AeB & BaC = assumption
  (ii) AeB   from (i) by rule 49 (Ch. 7)
  (iii) BaC   from (i) by rule 50 (Ch. 7)
  (iv) BeA   from (ii) by simple conversion
  (v)   CiB   from (iii) by accidental conversion
  (vi) BeA & CiB from (iv), (v), from two propositions to their conjunction
  (vii) CoA   from (vi) by *Ferio*
Therefore from first to last: AeB & BaC ∴ CoA   Q.E.D.

This completes my exposition of the most elementary parts of medieval syllogistic. In the next section we shall deal with complicating factors.

II. *Syllogistic tense logic*

Syllogistic as developed along the lines pursued in the preceding section can be tucked into a corner of the lower predicate calculus, and cannot therefore be expected to arouse much interest among modern logicians looking for new ideas (new to us!) from their medieval forebears. However the chief purpose of Section I was to place us in a position to examine certain aspects of medieval syllogistic which did not, unfortunately, find their way into the 'traditional' account of logic and which might reasonably be expected to interest not only antiquarians.

In Chapter Three, Section VI, attention was directed to the fact that the present tense was not the only tense of interest to medieval logicians. Neither was that interest prompted by purely logical considerations. For example, future contingent propositions were seen to generate problems both philosophical and theological. One such problem concerned the question of whether God's present knowledge about future human actions implies that no future human action will be performed freely. In the light of such concerns it is not surprising that medieval logic textbooks routinely included discussion of future-tensed propositions. Our earlier discussion focused on the appropriate way to set out the truth conditions of future- and past-tensed propositions, and in that respect our concern was primarily semantic. But of course nothing tells us more about the logic of non-present-tensed propositions than their role in valid inferences. It is to this syntactic topic that I wish to turn.

In Chapter Eight, Section III, we examined immediate inferences containing non-present-tensed propositions, for there we were concerned with rules of conversion for propositions whose subjects are ampliated to the past or the future. In this section our concern is with mediate inference, and in particular with rules for determining the validity or otherwise of syllogisms containing past- or future-tensed propositions. And since this was a matter of lively concern to medieval logicians it can come as no surprise that they were interested in the rules of conversion for such propositions, given the use to which, as we have seen, rules of conversion were put in establishing the validity or otherwise of syllogisms. The first detailed discussion of syllogisms with propositions ampliated to the past and the future was that by Ockham in his *Summa Logicae*. What is said in the remainder of this section is derived from that discussion. I shall attend to the first three figures only. No interesting additional logical principles appear to be involved in the fourth figure, in respect of premisses of which at least one is not present-tensed.

I shall deal with the three figures in turn. First the first. We have so far mentioned four first-figure syllogisms, *Barbara, Celarent, Darii*, and *Ferio*, each being immediately sanctioned by either the *dici de omni* or *dici de nullo* rule. There are two other valid first-figure syllogisms. For since the premisses of *Barbara* support a universal affirmative conclusion, they also, by a rule of subalternation, support a particular affirmative conclusion, and likewise the premisses of *Celarent* support not only a universal negative conclusion but also, by subalternation, a particular negative one. Each one of these six valid syllogisms remains valid if one or more of the propositions in each syllogism is transformed by replacing the present-tensed copula by a copula in another tense. But not every such transformation preserves validity. Our question now therefore concerns the identity of those rules of transformation that do preserve it.

The ampliative power of a non-present-tensed copula has to be taken into account here. Where the copula is past-tensed the subject supposits for what is or what was, and where it is future-tensed the subject supposits for what is or what will be. The rules of transformation that we are seeking specify how the subject is to be taken in a non-present-tensed proposition. For taken in one way a syllogism may be valid, but invalid if taken otherwise. Let us put some flesh on these bones.

Assuming the middle term to be common rather than singular, this rule holds: 'If the subject of the major premiss supposits for things which are, then the minor premiss should be neither future- nor past-tensed' (Ockham, *Summa Logicae*, III–1 17). The reason for this, briefly, is that otherwise the syllogism would not be regulated either by *dici de omni* or *dici de nullo*. Let us restrict consideration to the past tense (examples concerning the future tense can be dealt with along exactly the same lines), and use *Barbara* as an example, We shall consider why no conclusion can be drawn syllogistically from:

(i) Every (present) A was B & Every C was A.

The copula in the second conjunct ampliates the subject, but not the predicate, for the signification of the latter is restricted by the copula to what was A. Therefore the range of values of A in the putative major premiss is a set of present objects and the range of values of A in the putative minor premiss is a set of past objects. Hence no grounds are provided for concluding that anything whatever for which the first A supposits is identical with anything whatever for which the second A supposits. In effect the past-tensed copula in the second conjunct ensures that any syllogism of which (i) constitutes the set of premisses does not have a middle term, since two terms are middle terms in a given syllogism only if the ranges of values of the two terms are identical. The point can be brought out by writing the subject of the first conjunct as 'present-A' and the predicate of the second conjunct as 'past-A'. To conclude 'Every C was B' or 'Some C was B' from (i) is therefore to commit the fallacy of equivocation

But if the minor premiss is present-tensed then no such equivocation is committed. In each premiss A signifies what is A, and the rule *dici de omni* can be applied to draw the conclusions 'Every C was B' and 'Some C was B.' That is:

(ii) Every (present) A was B & Every C is A. Therefore every C was B

is valid because it falls under the rule: What is said [viz. that it was B] of a distributed subject [viz. what is now A] is true of everything [and therefore of every C] of which that distributed subject is truly predicated.

I have taken as my example an affirmative syllogism (that is, one with two affirmative premisses), but the same considerations apply to negative syllogisms (that is, syllogisms with a negative premiss). Thus:

(iii) No (present) A was B & Some C is A. Therefore some C was not B

is valid since it falls under the regulative principle that what is denied [viz. that it was B] of a distributed subject [viz. what is now A] is denied of everything [and therefore of some C] of which that distributed subject is truly predicated. And once again, and for the same reason as before, the syllogism is rendered invalid if the copula of the minor premiss is replaced by one which is not present-tensed.

Nothing said so far, however, permits the inference that unless the minor premiss of a first-figure syllogism is in the present tense, such a syllogism cannot have a past-tensed conclusion. The rule that for a past-tensed conclusion to be drawn the minor premiss must be in the present tense is applicable only to those cases where the past-tensed major premiss has a subject which is taken to stand for what is. For if the subject of the past-tensed major premiss is taken to stand for what was, then a conclusion can be drawn syllogistically if the minor premiss is past-tensed. The basic consideration here is the same as that invoked earlier, namely, the range of values of the subject of the major premiss must be identical with the range of values of the predicate of the minor. If, therefore, the subject of the major premiss is taken to signify what was, then the predicate of the minor must also be taken to signify what was and that signification is contrived by placing the copula of the minor premiss in the past tense. This prompts a question concerning the subject of the minor premiss, for given that the copula is past-tensed it follows that the subject is ampliated to signify either what is or what was. And we have to ask how that subject has to be taken if any syllogistic conclusion is to be drawn, or alternatively if one syllogistic conclusion rather than another is to be drawn. As we shall see, given that the subject of the past-tensed major premiss is taken to stand for what was, then a syllogistic conclusion can be drawn whether the subject of the minor premiss is taken to stand for what is or for what was. But how we take that minor subject certainly affects how we can take that term when it recurs in the conclusion, since it must be taken in the same way, whatever that way is, on both its occurrences. Thus this is valid:

(iv) Every (past) A was B & Every C was A. Therefore every C was B.

The *dici de omni* rule sanctions (iv) since in (iv) what is said [viz. that it was B] of the distributed subject [viz. what was A] is said of everything [and therefore of every C] of which that subject is truly predicated. If the subject of the minor premiss is taken to signify what was C, then that is how the subject in the conclusion should be taken. Otherwise the conclusion is not warranted by the premisses. Thus this is invalid:

(v) Every (past) A was B & Every (past) C was A. Therefore every (present) C was B.

It is clear that the premisses do not warrant any affirmative conclusion about a present C, for they do not imply even that any C now exists. And if (consistently with the premisses) no C exists, then, in accordance with the rule that an affirmative proposition with a subject which signifies nothing is false, the conclusion of (v) is false. And under certain conditions under which that conclusion is false the premisses are true. Hence the invalidity of (v). Similarly, this is invalid:

(vi) Every (past) A was B & Every (present) C was A. Therefore every (past) C was B.

In each of the kinds of case so far considered, from a pair of premisses of which at least one is not present-tensed a conclusion is drawn which has the same tense as the premiss which is not present-tensed. Let us now ask whether there can be a valid first-figure syllogism with a present-tensed conclusion though one of the premisses is not present-tensed. Let us suppose the major premiss present-tensed and the minor past. And we shall suppose that the subject of the major premiss is taken for what was, and the subject of the minor is taken for what is. Then a present-tensed conclusion can be drawn, as in this syllogism in *Barbara*:

(vii) Whatever was A is B & Whatever is C was A. Therefore whatever is C is B.

(vii) can readily be seen to be sanctioned by the rule *dici de omni*. Additionally if the subject of the minor premiss is a singular term instead of a common term taken to signify what is, the inference is valid. Thus this is valid where S is a singular term:

(viii) Whatever was A is B & S was A. Therefore S is B.

S might of course signify something which no longer exists, in which case the conclusion would be false. That would not affect the truth value of the minor premiss, since there the 'was' ampliates the subject to the present or the past. But it does affect the truth value of the major premiss. If S, which no longer exists, was A then it is not true that whatever was A is B, for S, not being anything, is not B. In that case the inference is not to a false conclusion from two premisses both of which are true. And therefore we have not set up a model which demonstrates the invalidity of (viii).

It has to be added, however, that even though the conclusion of a first-figure syllogism might be in the present tense while the minor premiss is not present-tensed, nevertheless if the major premiss is not present-tensed then neither can the conclusion be. The reason for this is that if the major premiss is past- or future-tensed then the predicate P of that premiss signifies what was or what will be. But if the conclusion is present-tensed then the predicate P in the conclusion must signify what is, and yet the premisses say nothing that permits any conclusion about what is P, even about whether any P exists. Thus this is invalid:

> (ix) Whatever is A was B & Whatever is C is A. Therefore whatever is C is B.

It is plain that the conclusion of (ix) should be:

> (x) Whatever is C was B.

We turn now to a consideration of second-figure syllogisms. Certain rules which are inapplicable to first-figure syllogisms are applicable to those of the second figure. For example, as regards first-figure syllogisms, we have just noted that if the major premiss is past-tensed then so also must be the conclusion. But in the second figure there are valid syllogisms containing two past-tensed premisses and a present-tensed conclusion. Ockham writes: 'When both premisses are past-tensed in the second figure and the subject of each of these supposits for things which are, there always follows a present-tensed conclusion, and not a past-tensed conclusion' (*Summa Logicae*, III–1 18). Thus this is valid:

> (xi) No (present) A was B & Some (present) C was B. Therefore some C is not A.

Ockham's argument for such syllogisms is as follows: 'From the major premiss and the opposite of the conclusion there follows the opposite of the minor premiss in the first figure.' The rule he here invokes is based on our rule 64 (Ch. 7). (xi) is equivalent to:

> (xii) No (present) A was B & Every C is A. Therefore no (present) C was B.

And (xii) is a valid first-figure syllogism in *Celarent* as can be demonstrated by using the rule *dici de nullo*. That is, what is denied [viz. that it was B] of a distributed subject [viz. what is A] is denied of everything [and therefore of every present C] of which that subject is truly predicated. The argument for (xi) may be presented as follows:

> (a)   No (present) A was B & Some (present) C was B
>   = assumption
> (b)   No (present) A was B
>   from (a) by rule 49 (Ch. 7)
> (c)   Some (present) C was B
>   from (a) by rule 50 (Ch. 7)

(d) Nothing which was B is A

        from (b) by simple conversion (see Ch. 7, Section. III)

(e) Nothing which was B is A & Some (present) C was B

        from (d), (c), from two propositions to their conjunction

(f) Some C is not A

        from (e) by *Ferio*

Therefore from first to last: (a) ∴ (f)   = (xi)   Q.E.D.

But, as just mentioned, from the premisses of (xi) no past-tensed conclusion follows. Ockham's argument in support of this claim is this:

> If it [the past-tensed] conclusion followed then from the opposite of the conclusion along with the major premiss there would follow the opposite of the minor premiss in the first figure, and consequently in the first figure under a major premiss in which the subject supposits for things which are there would be a minor premiss in the past tense. (*Summa Logicae*, III–1 18)

We have already in this section discussed the fallacy to which Ockham here alludes. Let us follow the argument through in relation to a suitably modified (xi). That is, we shall wrongly suppose this valid:

(xiii) No (present) A was B & Some (present) C was B. Therefore some (present) C was not A.

Applying rule 64 (Ch. 7) to (xiii) we derive this inference:

(xiv) No (present) A was B & Every (present) C was A. Therefore no (present) C was B.

This appears to have the form of a syllogism in *Celarent*, but the putative middle term does not in fact mediate between the other extremes. For A in the major premiss signifies what is, and in the minor what was. It is easy to construct counter-examples to (xiv). Let us suppose a set of two objects, O^1, O^2. At past time t^1 O^1 was grey and O^2 black. At t^2, between t^1 and the present, both objects were grey. Now O^1 is still grey but O^2 is white. We can now assert the following truths about our two objects: (a) No present grey object was black, (b) every present white object was grey, and (c) some present white object was black. (xiv), therefore, is invalid.

If, however, the subject in each premiss is taken to supposit for what was, then a past-tensed conclusion can validly be drawn. Thus this is valid:

(xv) No (past) A was B & Some (past) C was B. Therefore some (past) C was not A.

Applying rule 64 (Ch. 7) we derive:

(xvi) No (past) A was B & Every (past) C was A. Therefore no (past) C was B.

(xvi) is a valid syllogism in *Celarent* and can readily be derived from the rule *dici de nullo*. (xv) can be proved in the following way also:

(a) No (past) A was B & Some (past) C was B
      = assumption
(b) No (past) A was B
      from (a) by rule 49 (Ch. 7)
(c) Some (past) C was B
      from (a) by rule 50 (Ch. 7)
(d) No (past) B was A
      from (b) by simple conversion
(e) No (past) B was A & Some (past) C was B
      from (d), (c), from two propositions to their conjunction
(f) Some (past) C was not A
      from (e) by *Ferio*

Therefore from first to last: (a) ∴ (f)   = (xv)   Q.E.D.

Indeed even if the subject of the major premiss supposits for what was, and the subject of the minor supposits for what is, then, again, a past-tensed conclusion may follow. For example, this is valid:

(xvii) Every (past) A was B & No (present) C was B. Therefore no (present) C was A.

The proof of (xvii) is as follows:

(a) Every (past) A was B & No (present) C was B
      = assumption
(b) Every (past) A was B
      from (a) by rule 49 (Ch. 7)
(c) No (present) C was B
      from (a) by rule 50 (Ch. 7)
(d) No (past) B is C
      from (c) by simple conversion
(e) No (past) B is C & Every (past) A was B
      from (d), (b), from two propositions to their conjunction

(f) No (past) A is C
    from (e) by *Celarent*
(g) No (present) C was A
    from (f) by simple conversion

Therefore from first to last: (a) ∴ (g)　　= (xvii)　　Q.E.D.

We turn now to a consideration of third-figure syllogisms, and shall begin by supposing that both premisses are past-tensed and that the subjects are taken uniformly, that is, both are taken to supposit for what is or both for what was. In that case a past-tensed conclusion can validly be drawn. If the subjects of the premisses are not taken uniformly then no conclusion can be drawn syllogistically. An example should clarify this rule. The following is valid:

(xviii) No (present) A was B & Every (present) A was C.
        Therefore some (past) C was not B.

Applying rule 63 (Ch. 7) to (xviii) we reach:

(xix) Every (past) C was B & Every (present) A was C. Therefore some (present) A was B.

(xix) is a first-figure syllogism whose premisses are those of a syllogism in *Barbara*, and whose conclusion follows, by subalternation, from the conclusion of the syllogism in *Barbara*.

An alternative proof of (xviii) is the following:

(a) No (present) A was B & Every (present) A was C
    = assumption
(b) No (present) A was B
    from (a) by rule 49 (Ch. 7)
(c) Every (present) A was C
    from (a) by rule 50 (Ch. 7)
(d) Some (past) C is A
    from (c) by accidental conversion
(e) No (present) A was B & Some (past) C is A
    from (b), (d), from two propositions to their conjunction
(f) Some (past) C was not B
    from (e) by *Ferio*

Therefore from first to last: (a) ∴ (f)　　(=xviii)　　Q.E.D.

But it is clear that if the subject of the first premiss in (xviii) were taken for what was, then no conclusion could be drawn concerning the relation between B and C.

There are, also, valid third-figure syllogisms with a past-tensed conclusion, which do not have two past-tensed premisses. We can, for example, suppose the major premiss past-tensed and the minor present-tensed, with the subject of the major being taken for what is. Then a past-tensed conclusion can be drawn whose subject, like that of the major premiss, is taken for what is. Thus this is valid:

> (xx) Every (present) A was B & Every (present) A is C. Therefore some (present) C was B.

This can be proved as follows:

> (a) Every (present) A was B & Every (present) A is C
>   = assumption
> (b) Every (present) A was B
>   from (a) by rule 49 (Ch. 7)
> (c) Every (present) A is C
>   from (a) by rule 50 (Ch. 7)
> (d) Some (present) C is A
>   from (c) by accidental conversion
> (e) Every (present) A was B & Some (present) C is A
>   from (b), (d), from two propositions to their conjunction
> (f) Some (present) C was B
>   from (e) by *Darii*

Therefore from first to last: (a) ∴ (f)   (= xx)   Q.E.D.

It can also be shown that where the major premiss is present-tensed and the minor is past, a conclusion follows syllogistically. The reason for this can be displayed by 'reducing' such a third-figure syllogism to one in the first figure. Let us take as our third-figure syllogism:

> (xxi) No (present) A is B & Some (present) A was C. Therefore some (past) C is not B.

In the conclusion of (xxi) a past C is specified, for in the minor premiss the predicate stands for what was. Replacing the major premiss by the negation of the conclusion, and replacing the conclusion by the negation of the major premiss (see rule 65, Ch. 7), we reach:

> (xxii) Every (past) C is B & Some (present) A was C. Therefore some (present) A is B.

The validity of (xxii) can be demonstrated by reference to the rule *dici de omni*. We can also prove (xxi) in the customary way:

(a) No (present) A is B & Some (present) A was C
   = assumption
(b) No (present) A is B
   from (a) by rule 49 (Ch. 7)
(c) Some (present) A was C
   from (a) by rule 50 (Ch. 7)
(d) Some (past) C is A
   from (c) by simple conversion
(e) No (present) A is B & Some (past) C is A
   from (b), (d), from two propositions to their conjunction
(f) Some (past) C is not B
   from (e) by *Ferio*

Therefore from first to last: (a) ∴ (f)   (= xxi)   Q.E.D.

But the premisses of (xxi) do not support a past-tensed conclusion, for if the copula were past-tensed the predicate would stand for what was, though in the major premiss it stands for what is. The invalidity of (xxi) when thus modified is clearly displayed by reference to its equivalent first-figure syllogism. This latter is reached by replacing the major premiss of (xxi) by the negation of the modified conclusion, and replacing the modified conclusion by the negation of the major premiss. The result of this transformation of (xxi) is:

(xxiii) Every (past) C was B & Some (present) A was C .
   Therefore some (present) A is B.

It is plain that the premisses support the conclusion 'Some (present) A was B.' But that they do not support 'Some (present) A is B' follows from the fact that neither premiss in (xxiii) implies the present existence of anything which is B. And if, consistently with the premisses, no B exists, then the conclusion of (xxiii) is false. And on some consistent assumptions which are incompatible with the conclusion of (xxiii) the premisses are true. Therefore (xxiii) is invalid.

10

Conclusion

It will be clear from the sources quoted in this book that what I have presented is in large part a sketch of logic during the fourteenth century. The masters of that century were widely studied during the following one hundred and fifty years and numerous books were written transmitting their ideas and adding to them. Many of the additions were made when inferences were investigated with which the previously accepted rules of inference seemed unable to cope, unable either because the new inferences, if valid, were in conflict with old rules, or because the new inferences contained features and elements that placed them beyond the jurisdiction of the old rules. Other additions were made when questions arose concerning the application of accepted rules. For example, given rules involving conjunctive terms, questions were naturally raised about how a given occurrence of 'and' between categorematic terms is to be recognized as divisive or collective. Are there any ways of determining, on the basis of purely syntactic considerations, whether an 'and' is to be taken divisively or collectively?

Not surprisingly, medieval logic has been criticized for its 'damnable particularity'. But I should like to make two points in reply. First, concern for the particular is a price that is inevitably paid by any logician who takes the whole of a natural language as his object language, rather than taking an artificial language whose elements are introduced systematically item by item, with a duly assigned role.

Secondly, medieval logic was not solely concerned with the particular. The interest in the particular was, after all, a consequence of the desire to refine the presentation of the universal. Of course this led to a multiplication of low-level general rules. But there were also high-level rules of which the low-level ones were to be seen as so many specifications forced by the exigencies of the object language. In all this we should not lose sight of the fact that our logicians formulated and used a number of rules of a very high level of abstraction, which feature also in modern works on the propositional calculus—we looked at a number of such rules. And as regards the logic of terms, the basic rules of descent under terms covered by universal or particular quantifiers, or by signs of negation, are at a high level of logical abstraction and work well for a large proportion of the cases we are liable to encounter.

Nevertheless, to many it seemed as though the logic of the late medieval period was running practically out of control. There were simply too many rules, and no assurance that new ones might not be introduced indefinitely. The time was becoming ripe for change. The change came under the banner of the new humanism which was, by the late fifteenth century, beginning to take deep root in the universities. Turning to classical models for its inspiration it focused on an ancient concept of logic as a branch of rhetoric, the art of persuasion. One weapon in the armoury of the orator is skill at devising plausible arguments. And anyone seeking to persuade might find little or no help in the logic textbooks of the late medieval period. The fourteenth-century logicians were interested in rules of valid inference, and their textbooks offered no advice, except obliquely, on what was really a psychological problem of how to discover and present persuasive arguments. The logicians with whom we have been concerned did not lose sight of the position of logic as the art of arts and the science of sciences. For them its object was not persuasion, but truth. Their question was not: 'How do I find an argument that will persuade someone of the truth of a position I hold?', but 'How do I establish the validity of this argument?' And certainly to those not steeped in the medieval educational system the countless rules of logic must have seemed empty talk, and could hardly have been expected to make a disputed position seem more plausible.

Many of those rules are of no interest to us now, and many indeed are specific to Latin. But numerous rules that we have studied in this book are certainly of interest to the modern logician, and additionally the very approach to the analysis of propositions should be of interest. Particular mention must be made here, first, of the rules of descent and ascent by which medieval logicians gave an account of the signification of quantifiers, and secondly, of the rules concerning the order in which descent is to be made, by which logicians were able to deal successfully with inferences committing the quantifier shift fallacy. And in the light of new interest in tense logic, a reminder is here in order that it is a *renewed* interest, and that a substantial literature in that field was produced in the late medieval period. We studied some of the doctrines of syllogistic tense logic, and it is plain that those doctrines can be infused with a new vigour. But across the whole range of medieval logic there are to be found insights which can be put to work in contexts provided by modern logic. We should be grateful for those insights, and for the opportunity to give them new life in the modern science of logic.

Appendix
Biographical Register of Logicians Cited

I have listed only those logicians who are cited in this book. For biographical information on a much larger number of medieval logicians, see Kretzmann, N., Kenny, A., and Pinborg, J., eds., *The Cambridge History of Later Medieval Philosophy*, pp. 856–92.

ALBERT OF SAXONY 1316–90. Student at Prague, and at Paris where his master was John Buridan. MA Paris 1351. Taught at Paris 1351–62. Rector at Paris 1353. Co-founder and first rector of Vienna University 1365. Bishop of Halberstadt 1366–90.

BURIDAN, JOHN *c.*1295/1300–*c.*1360. MA Paris *c.*1320. Lecturer in Arts Faculty, Paris. Rector at Paris 1328, 1340.

BURLEY (or BURLEIGH), WALTER *c.*1275–1344/5. MA Oxford by 1301. Fellow of Merton College, Oxford, for at least four years till 1305. Theology student at Paris from before 1310. Doctorate of Theology, Paris, *c.*1320. Fellow of Sorbonne by 1324.

CRANSTON, DAVID *c.*1479–1512. Priest of the diocese of Glasgow. Matriculated at Paris 1495. Pupil of John Mair at College of Montaigu. Licensed in Arts 1499, and in same year began to teach Arts in Paris. Doctorate of Theology, Paris, 1512 (ten weeks before his death).

DOMINGO DE SOTO 1494/5–1560. Spanish Thomist. Studied under John Mair at Paris, and under Francisco de Vitoria. Entred Order of Preachers 1525. Taught at Salamanca.

GALBRAITH, ROBERT *c.*1483–1544. Pupil at Paris of John Mair and David Cranston. Licensed in Arts, Paris, 1503. Professor of Roman Law at College of Coqueret in Paris. Senator (i.e. lawyer member) of the College of Justice in Edinburgh.

LOKERT, GEORGE *c.*1485–1547. From Ayr, Scotland. Studied in Paris under John Mair and David Cranston. Licensed in Arts, Paris, 1505. Prior of the Sorbonne 1519. Doctorate of Theology, Paris, 1520. Rector of St Andrews University 1522–5. Overseer of Scots bursars of the Bishop of Muray's foundation, Paris, from *c.*1525. Dean of Glasgow 1534–47.

MAIR, JOHN *c.*1467–1550. From near Haddington, Scotland. Student at God's House (later Christ's College), Cambridge. Enrolled at University of Paris *c.*1491. MA Paris 1494. Taught arts at College of Montaigu from 1495. Doctorate of Theology, Paris, 1506. Taught theology at Sorbonne.

Principal of University of Glasgow 1518–23. Taught at St Andrews 1523–6. Taught theology at Paris 1526–31. Returned to St Andrews 1531, and taught arts and theology, becoming Provost of St Salvator's College, 1534. John Knox was one of his pupils there.

MANDERSTON, WILLIAM *c.*1485–1552. From Lothian area in Scotland. Enrolled at University of Glasgow 1503. MA 1506. Studied at Paris under John Mair. Professor of philosophy at College of Ste Barbe, Paris. Rector of Paris 1525. Rector of St Andrews 1530.

OCKHAM, WILLIAM *c.*1285–1347/9. Franciscan. Student at Oxford. Lectured at Oxford 1317–19. Summoned to Papal Court at Avignon 1324, charged with heresy. Fled from Avignon 1328, and was given asylum by German Emperor, Ludwig of Bavaria. Ockham excommunicated. Shortly before his death he apparently sought to have the excommunication rescinded, but it is unknown whether he signed the formula of submission.

PAUL OF VENICE *c.*1369–1429. Entered Augustinian Convent of S. Stefano, Venice. Studied at Padua. At Oxford 1390–*c.*1393. Doctor of Arts and Theology at Padua 1408. Rector and Vicar-General of Augustinians 1409–10. Ambassador of Venice on several occasions. Rector of University of Siena 1428. His *Logica Magna* (1397–8) is an encyclopaedia of logic.

PETER OF SPAIN (Pope John XXI) d.1277. Studied arts at Paris. Professor of medicine at Siena 1245–9. Dean of Lisbon and Archdeacon of Braga 1250. Archbishop of Braga 1273. Cardinal Archbishop of Tusculum. Elected Pope 1276.

WILLIAM OF SHERWOOD *c.*1200/10–1266/72. Student at Oxford. Master at Oxford 1252. Treasurer of Lincoln from 1254/8.

Bibliography

Albert of Saxony, *Perutilis Logica* (Venice, 1522; reprinted Olms Verlag, Hildesheim, 1974).

Ashworth, E. J., *Language and Logic in the Post-Medieval Period* (Dordrecht, 1974).

—— 'Multiple quantification and the use of special quantifiers in early sixteenth century logic', *Notre Dame Journal of Formal Logic*, 19 (1978), 599–613.

Boehner, P., *Collected Articles on Ockham*, ed. E. M. Buytaert (Louvain, 1958).

—— *Medieval Logic: an Outline of its Development from 1250–c.1400* (Manchester, 1966).

Broadie, A., *George Lokert: Late-Scholastic Logician* (Edinburgh, 1983).

—— *The Circle of John Mair: Logic and Logicians in Pre-Reformation Scotland* (Oxford, 1985).

—— (ed. and tr.), *Paul of Venice, Logica Magna*, Pt. II, fasc. 3 (Oxford, forthcoming).

Cranston, David, *Sequuntur abbreviationes omnium parvorum logicalium collecte a magistro Anthonio Ramirez de Villascusa cum aliquibus divisionibus terminorum eiusdem necnon cum tractatu terminorum magistri Davidis Cranston ab eodem correcto* (Paris, c.1513).

Del Punta, F. and Adams, M. McC. (eds. and trs.), *Paul of Venice, Logica Magna*, Pt. II, fasc. 6 (Oxford, 1978).

Domingo de Soto, *Introductiones Dialectice* (Burgis, 1529).

Fernando de Enzinas, *Primus Tractatus Summularum* (Compluti, 1523).

Freddoso, A. J. and Schuurman, H. (trs.), *Ockham's Theory of Propositions: Part II of the Summa Logicae* (Notre Dame, 1980).

Galbraith, Robert, *Quadrupertitum in oppositiones, conversiones, hypotheticas et modales magistri Roberti Caubraith omnem ferme difficultatem dialecticam enodans* (Paris, 1516).

Geach, P. T. *Reference and Generality* (3rd edn. London, 1980).

—— *Logic Matters* (Oxford, 1981).

Henry, D. P., *Medieval Logic and Metaphysics* (London, 1972).

John Buridan, *Consequentie* (Paris, 1498).

—— *Sophismata* (Paris, 1493).

Kesler, Andreas, *De Consequentia Tractatus Logicus* (Wittebergae, 1623).

Kneale, William and Martha, *The Development of Logic* (Oxford, 1962).

Kretzmann, N., *William of Sherwood's Introduction to Logic* (University of Minnesota Press, 1966).

—— *William of Sherwood's Treatise on Syncategorematic Words* (University of Minnesota Press, 1968).

—— 'Medieval logicians on the meaning of the *propositio*', *Journal of Philosophy*, 67 (1970), 767–87.

—— (ed. and tr.), *Paul of Venice, Logica Magna*, Pt. I, fasc. 1 (Oxford, 1979).

Kretzmann, N., Kenny, A., Pinborg, J. (eds.), *The Cambridge History of Later Medieval Philosophy* (Cambridge, 1982).

Lokert, George, *Sillogismi* (Paris, *c.*1522).

—— *Termini* (Paris, *c.*1523).

—— *De Oppositionibus* (Paris, 1523).

Łukasiewicz, J., *Aristotle's Syllogistic from the Standpoint of Modern Formal Logic*, (2nd edn. Oxford, 1957).

Mair, John, *Inclitarum artium ac sacre pagine doctoris acutissimi magistri Johannis Maioris . . . Libri quos in artibus in collegio Montis Acuti Parisius regentando compilavit* (Paris, 1506).

—— *Introductorium in Aristotelis dialecticen totamque logicen Magistri Johannis Maioris* (Paris, 1521).

Manderston, William, *Tripartitum epithoma doctrinale et compendiosum in totius dyalectices artis principia a Guillelmo Manderston Scoto nuperrime collectum* (Paris, 1520).

Moody, E. A., *Truth and Consequence in Medieval Logic* (Westport, 1976).

Nuchelmans, G., *Late-Scholastic and Humanist Theories of the Proposition* (Amsterdam, 1980).

Paul of Venice, *Logica* (also called *Logica Parva*), (Venice, 1472; reprinted Olms Verlag, Hildesheim, 1970).

—— *Logica Magna* (Venice, 1499). See also Broadie, A. (forthcoming); Kretzmann, N. (1979); Del Punta, F. and Adams, M. McC. (1978).

Peter of Spain, *Tractatus* (also called *Summule Logicales*), ed. L. M. de Rijk (Assen, 1972).

Prior, A. N., *Formal Logic* (2nd edn. Oxford, 1962).

—— *The Doctrine of Propositions and Terms*, eds. Geach, P., and Kenny, A. (London, 1976).

Tartaretus, Peter, *Expositio in Summulas Petri Hispani* (Paris, 1520).

Vives, Juan Luis, *In Pseudodialecticos*, ed. Fantazzi, C. (Leiden, 1979).

Walter Burley (or Burleigh), *De Puritate Artis Logicae Tractatus Longior, with a revised edition of the Tractatus Brevior*, ed. Boehner, P. (New York, 1955).

William of Ockham, *Logica Magna*, ed. Boehner, P. (New York, 1975).

William Sherwood, *Introductiones in Logicam*, ed. Grabmann, M. (Sitzungsberichte der Bayerischen Akademie der Wissenschaften Phil.-hist. Abteilung 1937, 10). Verlag der Bayerischen Akademie der Wissenschaft.

—— *Syncategoremata*, ed. O'Donnell, J. R. *Medieval Studies*, 3, (1941), 44–93.

Index